To the strongest warriors, and the sharpest businessmen of the lands of Rajasthan and Gujarat when combined, we call then the Thar Express of the World.

Contents

Contents

Preface

The Thar Express:

Culinary History of Rajasthan and Gujarat

"*Set against the backdrop of the Thar and the Kutch, the region is regarded as the beautiful land of vibrant colors, wonderful palaces, attractive architecture, mesmerizing history, enchanting dances and tasty cuisines.*"

Dr Anshumali Pandey

CHAPTER ONE

Introduction

Set against the backdrop of the Thar and the Kutch, the region is regarded as the beautiful land of vibrant colors, wonderful palaces, attractive architecture, mesmerizing history, enchanting dances and tasty cuisines. These western states face the problem of scarcity of water and green vegetables.

Apart from this the climatic condition and the frequent war conditions also influenced the local cuisine. Long lasting food, not requiring any heating, evolved because of the frequent wars fought by the state. Thus, the people have evolved a cooking style and diverse food habits that slowly developed into a unique cuisine that has taken up the influence of their long-line of royal heritage and the unavailability of resources brought upon by the arid conditions of the area. Traditional food of Rajasthan is very much in demand of tourists throughout the year.

Gujarat is one of the most progressive states in the country. Lead by powerful modern leaders, the development of the state is unstoppable and non comparable. There are many beautiful places to visit in Gujarat. These could be weekend getaways or a long vacation. People of Gujarat are friendly and the food is delicious. Each of the districts has the taste of their own.

While traveling from North towards south, one shall find more sweetness to the food. People in Gujarat prefer sweetness similar to their nature. People are good, places are worth stay, the cuisine is worth having; all of these qualities make Gujarat a must see; must visit place; a place to be.

Part A: Rajasthan

Culinary History of Rajasthan

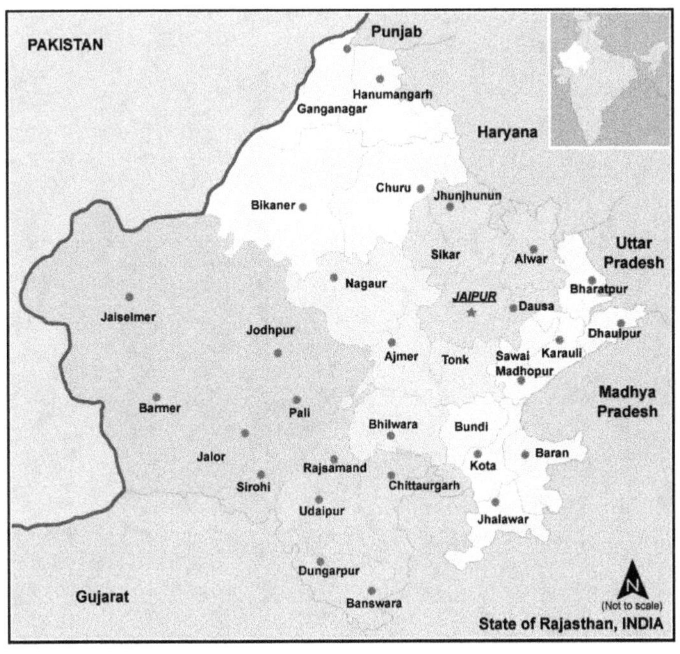

CHAPTER TWO

Geography of Rajasthan

Rajasthan is situated in the north-western part of India. It is the largest Indian state by area and the seventh largest by population. Rajasthan is located on the northwestern side of India, where it comprises most of the wide and inhospitable Thar Desert (also known as the "Rajasthan Desert" or "Maru-kantar" or "Great Indian Desert") and shares a border with the Pakistani provinces of Punjab to the northwest and Sindh to the west, along the Sutlej-Indus river valley. The rest it is bordered by five other Indian states: Punjab to the north; Haryana and Uttar Pradesh to the northeast; Madhya Pradesh to the southeast; and Gujarat to the southwest. The capital city is Jaipur. The oldest chain of fold mountains- the Aravali Range splits the state into two geographical zones- desert at one side and forest belt on the other. The Mount Abu is the only hill station of the state and houses the Guru Shikhar Peak which is the highest peak. This place is famous for Dilwara Jain Temples.

The topography includes rocky terrain, rolling sand dunes, wetlands, barren tracts or land filled with thorny scrubs, river-drained plains, plateaus, ravines and wooded regions. All the rivers are mostly situated in the eastern part of the state. Chambal and Luni are the main rivers quenching the thirst of this state along with few other small rivers like Kali, Banas, Banganga, Parvati, Gambhiri, Mahi, Kakni, Jokham, Sabarmati, Katli, Sabi and Mantha. The State's scorching and dry summers and its parched landscape are undergoing significant changes because of the developmental effort that have led to the spread of the Indira Gandhi canal.

A Brief History of Rajasthan

Rajasthan, the land of Raja-Maharajs has witnessed a glorious history, which dates back to the ancient times. There is an interesting legend attached to the history of Rajasthan. It is believed that ages ago when Lord Rama (heroic figure in Hindu Mythology) was about to fire an arrow towards Lanka where his consort Goddess Sita was imprisoned by the demon king Ravana, other Gods requested him to refrain from doing so. However, once the arrow was drawn it could not be taken back, so Lord Rama released the arrow at a distant sea. As a result, all the water evaporated from the sea and from it rose the great Indian Thar Desert, Rajasthan.

According to archaeological reports, the settlements in Rajasthan began during the Indus Valley Civilization (2500 BC). It is believed that the civilization declined due to several factors such as earthquake and invasions. Later the trade link between Europe and Asia came as a blessing to Rajasthan as it is during this period that the settlements were re-established. The Aryans occupied the Dundhmer region of Rajasthan and settled there in 2000 BC. Mina and Bhil tribes were the first inhabitants of Rajasthan. Constant fights between these two tribe resulted in several small kingdoms. Next came the Maurya dynasty, which ruled over Rajasthan till 400 AD.

The great king Ashoka was one of the kings of the Maurya dynasty who, after seeing the horrible results of the war took to Buddhism to understand life better. Thereafter the Guptas established their supremacy in the 4th century and ruled for 300 years. Famous for their bravery, the Rajputs ruled Rajasthan from the 7th century AD. But infighting amongst themselves eventually split them into 36 splinters, and ever since, Rajasthan has been referred to as the Land of Rajputs. 1200 AD saw the rise of the Muslim rulers who were later defeated by Marathas in 1707. Finally, British rule was established in 1817, and came to an end in 1947 when India gained Independence.

CHAPTER FOUR

Social life of Rajasthanis

The people of Rajasthan are as diverse and colorful as the state itself. The dominating populations of the Rajasthan are the Rajputs. The state is also popularly known as 'Land Of Rajputs' which means the 'son of the king' and is believed that they belong to the warrior clan or the descendants of the Ksatriyas of Vedic India. Indeed, the state draws its name from this community. Since ancient times, the profession of a person was the deciding factor of his caste. The tradition has been modified in modern times and now the caste is decided by the family in which a child is born. One can say it has become a birth based caste system.

The caste does not restrict an individual to choose a profession of his own. In terms of caste structure, the Brahmans (highest caste) are subdivided into many gotras (lineages) who carry out rituals and holy practices; the Rajputs noted for their bravery are classified into various castes and sub castes where the Gurjar Pratiharas are supposed to be the earliest of the Rajput clan. Some of the other Rajput clan includes the Sisodias, Rathors, Chauhans, Kachawahas, Bhattis, Panwars and Solankis, while the

Mahajans (trading caste) are subdivided into a bewildering number of groups.

In the north and west the Jats (peasant caste) and Gujars (herding caste) are among the largest agricultural communities. In the eastern part of the state, those groups include the Mina (and the related Meo), most of whom are farmers; the Banjara, who have been known as traveling traders and artisans; and the Gadia Lohar, another historically itinerant tribe, who traditionally have made and repaired agricultural and household implements. The Bhil, one of the oldest communities in India, generally inhabit southern Rajasthan and have a history of possessing great skill in archery. The Grasia and Kathodi also largely live in the south, mostly in the Mewar region. Sahariya communities are found in the southeast, and the Rabari, who traditionally are cattle breeders, live to the west of the Aravallis in west-central Rajasthan.

Atleast 12% of the total population of Rajasthan is constituted by the tribal people. Some of the major tribes of Rajasthan are the Bhils, Minas, Lohars, Garasias and Sahariyas. Udaipur is mainly occupied by the Bhils tribal community and districts like Jaipur and Madhopur are inhabited by the Minas. Garasias and Sahrias tribes belong to the Sirohi and Kota district. The lohars are nomads who found their home in Udaipur. The Sahariyas inhabit the jungles of Shahbad, Jhalawar, Sawai Madhopur, Dungarpur and Udaipur.

CHAPTER FIVE

Climate of Rajasthan

Being the driest region in India, the royal state experiences a tropical desert climate. Rajasthan features extreme temperatures in both summer and winter.

The presence of the desert makes the summer days very hot and nights very cold. In the dessert the nighttime temperatures in winters can reach -1°C, as can be witnessed in Churu. Jaisalmer and Barmer district at any time of the year. The summer season extends from April to June where the maximum daytime temperature varies from 280C to 45°C. Prevailing winds are from the west and sometimes carry dust storms (we call them aandhi). In day time this wind is called —Looh.

The winter season falls in the between the months of December to March in Rajasthan, where the days are more or less pleasant, and is the best time to visit this state. The night experiences harsh cold climate where the temperature may fall below 00C. The monsoon occurs mainly in the eastern region during the month of July to September, so this area is fertile and suitable for growing crops.

CHAPTER SIX

The Staple Food and Agriculture of Rajasthan

The State has only 10% land useful for farming. In spite of this the agricultural sector has long been the mainstay of Rajasthan's economy. It accounts for about one-fourth of the state's economic output, employing about two-thirds of the state's working population. Despite scanty and scattered rainfall, nearly all types of crops are grown, including pearl millet in the desert area, sorghum around Kota, and mainly corn (maize) and ground nuts around Udaipur.

Wheat, barley and pulses (such as peas, beans, and lentils), sugarcane, and oilseeds (Rape and mustard) are fairly well distributed in the plains that are drained by the rivers and streamlets owing to the alluvial and clay soil deposits. The main source of irrigation is wells and tanks. The Indira Gandhi Canal irrigates northwestern Rajasthan.

Rice is grown in the irrigated areas of both the southeast and the northwest. The hilly tracts of the Aravali are characterized by the black, lava soils that sustain the growth of cotton and Isabgol. This area is also suited for the growth of some spice plants, especially red, hot chilies. These chilies give Rajasthan its distinct flavor.

Other spices are cumin seeds and fenugreek. Cotton and tobacco are important cash crops. Apart from this crops an assortment of fruits and vegetables are also grown in Rajasthan in the local gardens and some fertile regions. These fruits include oranges, guavas, lemon, pomegranates and mangoes.

Due to odd and harsh climatic condition the folk of Rajasthan could not cultivate vast fields of food, they became champions of animal husbandry, nurturing and maintaining hordes of cattle despite the scarcity of grazing land. They found that lentils and legumes flourished in the semi-fertile land northeast of the Aravallis, and they made them an integral part of their diet. They discovered desert berries and created magnificent dishes from them. Spices grow well even in the arid soil of this land, and are more pungent and potent because of it, making them the star ingredients in most dishes and imparting a wholly distinct flavour to the food.

Rajasthan has a large livestock population and is a major wool-producing state. It also is a source of camels and draft animals of various breeds. Apart from farming they are also engaged in animal husbandry and activities like handicrafts in brass, silver, lacquer, pottery, wood, and leather.

CHAPTER SEVEN

The Famous Rajasthani Cookery

The common households used the simplest of cooking methods to prepare the food. Each home was equipped with a basic stone or clay stove (angithi) fuelled by wood and coal called an. In some of the more rural areas and amongst the nomadic tribes, food was cooked on stoves made of hardened mud (chullah) and cow dung cakes were used.

Sometimes a flat slab of stone was placed on blazing coal. Once hot, it would work as a grill and food placed upon it would be roasted. Since fuel like wood and coal was a rare and expensive commodity and was often not available for days, food had to have a long shelf life and needed to be easily edible without requiring any heating or further preparation. These durable recipes were also preferred because of the necessity of travel for the men folk, who were away from home for several days at a stretch, mostly for economic purposes like work or trading and sometimes for recreational pastimes like hunting.

Yet another reason was the constant state of internal conflict and war within Rajasthan as Rajputs eagerly engaged in frequent battles for land and honour. These battles often meant food supply routes were cut off, especially during sieges, so large quantities of food that could be preserved for long periods of time were prepared beforehand.

Geographically, the state experiences scarcity of water and due to which fresh green vegetables are least available, which in turn has influenced the cuisine of this land. As a result, most of the delicacies of Rajasthan are cooked with the minimum quantity of water. Milk and buttermilk are used in generous quantities in the preparation of Rajasthani food.

The cooking mediums that are commonly used are desi ghee, mustard oil and rape seed oil.

Only the Rajputs used to lavish meat, but not frequently and usually preferred to keep a vegetarian and lacto-vegetarian diet. Chicken is uncommon and is rarely used ingredient, Goat and lamb meat is widely used but they were still a bit of a secondary preference.

Another form of an outdoor kitchen is the khad (deep pit) style of cooking of Rajasthan. When hunting wildlife was not considered a violation of animal rights, members of the royal family would set out on a shikar (hunting), which were hunted during pastime and was a passion of the royal Rajputs. Cooking the hunted animals or game cooking was considered as a kind of royality. In the khad style of cooking large leaves and mitti (wet earth) were used in lieu of a utensil. The heat source at the base of the pit was by burning charcoal covered with dry twigs and cow dung to provide the heat. The marinated shikar was tightly wrapped in the leaves, which were then coated with mitti and placed in the pit which was then covered with sand. After a passage of time the pit was dug up, the dried-up mitti crust was broken and the deliciously aromatic preparation, cooked in its own juices, was ready to be eaten. One such creation is the unique Junglee Maas by the Maharaja of Salwar 'Khad khasrgosh' (Hare or rabbit meat cooked in a pit), 'Khad ka pind' or 'Khad maans' (delicacy of chicken) by Hada Rajput royal family. The hunted game was simply cooked in clarified butter, salt and plenty of hot red chilies due to the scarcity of exotic ingredients in the kitchen of hunting camp.

Other non-vegetarian dishes include 'soola' or barbecued meats, marinated with a local vegetable, Murg ko khaato (chicken cooked in a curd gravy), soor santh ro sohito (pork with millet dumplings). Apart from these Lal maans and Maans ke sule and and Safed Maas by Kachchhawadas of Jaipur are also on the top list of meat delicacy.

Despite such popularity of the meat dishes the vast majority of inhabitants have always been staunch vegetarians. Vegetable and fruit produces include Cluster beans (Gawar ki phalli), Mateera (Kind of gourd resembling watermelon, Singhara (water chestnut), Kawkari (kakri or kakdi) –a type of cucumber, also called pahadi kheera, it's a type of cucumber.

Every other ethnic group in Rajasthan abstained from meat and relies on dairy products as both the base for curries and for cooking. The Jains, Marwaris, Bishnois and Maheshwaris abstain from most root vegetables, and avoided onion and garlic, which are integral parts of most Rajasthani cooking.

In the absence of a variety in vegetables, hardy grains like Bajra (pearl millet), wheat and gram became staples, along with moth, soya bean and ground nuts. Dried lentils as well as beans from local plants like Ker, Sangri etc are utilized in Rajasthani cuisine quite liberally.

Spices like dry red chilies, cumin, coriander, custard, fennel, fenugreek, sesame seeds, garlic, coconut and kaachri (Berry used as a souring agent and meat tenderizers- Cucamelons). Maithania town near Jodhpur is famous for its red fiery chilli – called Maithania mirch or Lal Badshah Gram flour is one main ingredient used by the people to make delicacies like 'khata', 'ghatta ki sabzi' and 'pakodi'. Mangodi and Papad forms a part of their daily meal and it is made of powdered lentils. The most commonly used grains are Bajra and corn with which they make rotis, 'rabdi' and 'kheechdi'. Jalebis and Fafda are usually taken along with a glass of milk in the morning.

Fruits like Sita-phal (custard apple), oranges, guavas, lemon, pomegranates and mangoes, datepalm, karonda, lasoda or gonda (Indian glue berry), are also part of daily diet.

Soup also form a part of their daily lunch which is made of legumes and alternately flavored with red chili peppers, yoghurt or milk and sometimes a vegetable such as lady finger, jackfruit, brinjal, mustard or fenugreek leaf.

Chutneys made of spices like turmeric; coriander mint and garlic are prepared and are hot and spicy. Various types of chutneys are also an integral part of the cuisine of Rajasthan. Most of these are made from local spices like turmeric, coriander, garlic and mint.

Dal baati churma and Bikaneri bhujia have garnered both national and international popularity among foodies.

Another interesting indigenous practice is that of dungar cooking, wherein the prepared food is placed in a vessel (usually a bronze or copper pot) and a small container with a hot piece of coal is kept in the centre of the dish inside the vessel. Hot ghee is then poured onto the coal and the dish is covered for 30 minutes, giving the dish an intoxicating smoky flavour and aroma.

During summers, an appetizing and refreshing drink Aanch is very popular. It is made of pureed roasted mango pulp and spices.

CHAPTER EIGHT

The Amazing Sweets of Rajasthan

Native Rajasthanis have a unique style of coupling the sweet dishes with the main (bread/roti/puri) course instead of or in addition to vegetables or meat. Halwa - Puri for example makes a famous combination. A great use of clarified butter (ghee) characterizes the sweets.

Chashni (caramel) based Halwas and Chakkis are a must on most festive occasion. A variety of dal ka halwas are made using lentils such as Moong dal ka halwa, Semoina (Sooji ka Halwa) or Besan ka hlawa (Chakki). Ajmer is famous for its Sohan Halwa.

Jaisalmer is also known for the many varieties of laddus (sweet balls) prepared commonly in the households. Motichur ka Laddu, Besan ka Laddu, Dal ka Laddu and the unique Gaund ka Laddu eaten mostly in winter months due to the heat it imparts to the system are the state's specialties. Gotma (small sugar dipped boondis which are mashed) is common in almost all occasions.

A number of diary products are also effectively used in making desserts. Kheer is a milk-based sweet dish. Kheer is cooked in variations such as with the more common rice or with vermicelli (Seviyan Kheer). Makhane ka Kheer and Jhajharia are also diary based recipes cooked only by the natives of the state. Ghevar (a specialty of Jaipur) of is probably the most intriguing of sweets prepared in the state. It is a must have on Makar Shankaranti, a festival that usually falls around the 14th of January every year.

The Rabri topped Jalebi of Rajasthan is legendary. Malpuas of Pushkar, Kalakand and Diljani of Udaipur, Mishri Mawa and Imarti of Ajmer, Balushahi and Makhan bade of Kishangarh, Chiwde ke pede of Pillani, Mawa Kachori of Bikaner have claimed the hearts of international tourists.

CHAPTER NINE

The Royal Culinary Heritage of Rajasthan

The royal households of Rajasthan (called rajthikanas or rajgharanas) were famed for their lavish and extravagant lifestyles. It was in the magnificent kitchens of these royal families that some of the richest and most flavourful dishes find their origins. Each royal gharana has a huge rasowara (kitchen) that usually employed a minimum of 10 to 12 chefs, called khansamas, whose primary job was to cook new and innovative dishes using different ingredients, especially game meats using dry fruits. Game meats included wild hare, wild boar, venison, duck, pheasant, rabbit, quail and even camel. Laal Maas, Govind Gattas, Doodh ke Samose, Kaleji ka Raita, Khad Khargosh, Khargosh ki Mokal, Lahsoon ki Kheer were also a part of the festivity. More than hundreds of dishes were made and served during any kind of royal festival. These were presented in elaborate vessels made from the rarest of precious materials.

The Royal Thali: A traditional Rajasthani Thali depicts a brilliant play of gourmet preparations on a plate of epic proportions. A big Thali meticulously arranged with small bowls all around, and each bowl consists of delicious preparations displaying numerous dishes. It is a complete menu with snacks, main course, side dishes, sweets and beverages.

<u>The dishes may be:</u>

Breads- Rotis, Pooris, Kachauris, Bati and Parathas made of wheat flour, besan, bajra, makka and jowar.

Rice- Plain rice, pulao

Dal- Besan kadhi, Gatte ki sabji, Moong dal, Mixed dal, Amras ki kadhi, Papad ki sabji, Ker sangria,

Non- vegetarian dishes- Laal maans, Safed maans, Banjari gosht, Bhuna kukda, Khad khargosh, Sula

Accompaniments- Chick pea salads, Papad, Fried chilies, Lahsun chutney, Red chilli chutney

Beverages- Lassi, Chhaans, Thandai, Raita

Sweets- Imarti, Malpua, Rasgulla and Moong dal halwa, Mawa misri, Ghewar, Gond ke laddoo, Churma laddoo.

CHAPTER TEN

Rajasthani Kitchen Equipments and Utensils

Rajasthani Kitchen Equipments and Utensils:

- Tikra: This is a clay pot that is typically used for making a dal called tikri ki dal. The much desired earthy flavour of the dal is obtained in this manner.
- Chullah: In the olden days, stoves were made out of mud and cow dung was the most commonly used fuel. The low flame of the chulah would cook the food and the flavour of the spices would be more pronounced.
- Sigri: This is an open barbecue griller used for grilling kebabs such as maans ke sooley.

Very little 'special' equipment would be needed to prepare your Rajasthani cuisine. Pots and pans those are non-stickyof course as they make the best utensils for simply any type of cooking. Moreover, using wooden stirrers in place of stainless steel ones is the best choice always. The traditional Rajasthani breads such as chapattis, parathas and rotis are all made using the tawa. Karahi is another deep frying pot which looks quite like a Chinese wok but it is heavier and deeper than the former. The karahi makes a great alternative for ordinary deep frying recipes. Commonly the meat dishes are prepared in the karahi. Other equipments used are karchhi, palta, deg, lota, mortar pestle etc. Meat pieces are roasted after being pierced in iron skewers.

Festive Dishes of Rajasthan

Amrud ki sabji: This is an exquisite delicacy of guava simmered in a tangy tomato and yoghurt masala.

Dal Bati Churma: Bati is flaky round bread baked under a mound of firewood or cow dung cakes. They can also be steamed. Batis are accompanied by Panch Kutti Dal and Churma. A part of unsalted dough batis are deep fried, crushed, mixed with sugar or jaggary, form small laddoo bals alled Churma loddoo.

Badi ka saag: It is sun-dried moth-lentil dumplings mixed with spices and cooked dry

Bajra roti: Crispy flat bread made of millet flour is one of the most favored edibles for Rajasthanis. Bajra rotis, soaked in clarified butter, are often matched with lehsun ki chutney, Ker Sangri ka Saag, Gwaar phali ka saag, Rajasthani Khaata, and even sweet jaggary.

Bajre ki Roti: It is a crisp roti paired with a natural onion and Lahsun ki Chutney

Banjari Gosht: It is a hot spicy preparation of mutton and curd, the shining reddish brown colour exihibits the royal taste.

Bejad ki roti: It is wonderful flat bread made of a mix of chick pea and barley flour, Bejad rotis are highly nutritious. High on fibre, and low on carbohydrates.

Bhedawi Puri: Bhedawi Puri is the favorite fried flat breads. It is made of urad daal (black gram lentils) flour, fennel and nigella seeds. The crunchiness of Bhedawi puris make them ideal for the tea-time snacks as well.

Bhuna Kukda: Marinated chicken is cooked in a mixture of spices until it gets tender and then sprinkled with coriander leaves.

Bina Pani ki Roti: Made with just boora (ground sugar), ghee, milk and flour. it is pressed into a flat roundel by hand, and cooked on a mitti ka tawa called a khejdi, often decorated with saffron, cardamom seeds and raisins.

Chilla: Generally Besan ka chilla is a very common street food from Rajasthan. It can be made from besan or moong dal. Paste of these are spread on tawa like dosas and cooked on a hot plate and stuffed with grated paneer and folded over to a half moon. It is served hot with garlic chutney.

Dilkushar: Also known as 'Mohanthal' or 'Besan ki Chakki', Dilkushar is made by roasting besan (gram flour) and mawa in copious amount of ghee. Sugar syrup is poured over the gram flour mixture and allowed to set. Once it sets, cardamom and chopped dried fruits are sprinkled on. This fudgy confection is cut into squares, and has a chewy texture with sweet grainy flavour.

Doodh pheni: Highly garnished Sewaiyan kheer

Gatte ki Sabzi: Popular and all-time favorite Rajasthani (Marwari) recipe with gram flour dumplings simmered in a tangy gravy made of buttermilk and spices. It is eaten with rotis/rotla (Indian bread) or rice.

Ghevar: Made in large quantities on the festival of Teej, Ghevar is one of Rajasthan's quintessential sweet delicacies. It is disc shaped and has a crispy but porous texture. It is made of corn flour, fried in ghee (clarified butter) and then infused with sugar syrup.

Jhanajariya: Small pedas made of corn, milk, ghee and sugar and garnished with raisins and nuts

Kachori: Small golden brown discs of flour filled with spiced lentils or more famously, spiced onions. Kachoris are served with various kinds of chutneys.

Kalmi Vada: This crispy and crunchy snack delicacy made of batter of chana dal, onion, dhania seeds, chillies and other ingredients savoured with chilli or mint chutneys forms a perfect tea-time snack.

Khad ka pinda: This preparation is associated with wild animals. In this case, a rabbit is marinated and wrapped in a jute cloth. It is then covered with clay and cooked embedded in the earth with simmering wood charcoals on top.

Khad: A multi – tiered cake of lamb mince and phulka – a magnificent meal in itself. Khad means a hole in the ground. Originally, the 'cake' was baked in a hole in the ground with charcoals and hot sand providing the heat.

Khichra: It is a porridge of millets and moth lentils that are cooked along with water, a little spice and some ghee in combination with either jaggary or karhi form a staple part of Rajasthani diet.

Khoba roti: Khoba roti, in short, is the elaborated version of regular whole-wheat chapatti. The surface of the Khoba chapatti is made uneven by pinching it lightly with fingers. All this is done to increase the absorbing quality of the bread, which would later be poured with a great quantity of clarified butter.

Laal Maas: A traditional Rajasthani meat recipe, Laal Maas literally means 'red meat'. A curry is made by marinating lamb pieces with ground red chilies and other spices that give it a red tinge and spicy flavor.

Laapsi: It is prepared with broken wheat (dalia) browned in a pan containing a small quantity of ghee and then sweetened with sugar or jaggary and dressed with saffron and dried nuts and raisins. It is a special sweet dish of Rajasthanis.

Lahsun ki chutney: A saucy and spicy preparation or garlic and onion.

Maans kay sooley: This dish is usually eaten as an appetizer. Thin slices of lamb are firstly marinated overnight in buttermilk and spices. They are then skewered and cooked on a charcoal grill.

Machhli Jaisamandi: Tender pieces of fish are marinated in a green paste which is then fried and cooked in gravy full of spices and silky creamy texture.

Makki ka soweta: This is a spicy combination of corn and lamb in which lamb is cooked with yoghurt and various spices and grated corn and milk is added.

Malpuwa: It is a soft pancake dipped in sugar syrup or thickened milk (rabri) and served as a sweet.

Mirchi vada: The Jodhpur mirchi bada, a spicy chilli cutlet made of chilli and potato stuffing is a popular Rajasthani snacks item that goes along well with tamarind chutney, mint chutney or tomato sauce.

Missi roti: This is avery famous bread prepared by kneading gram flour, wholewheat flour, chopped onions, and green chillies into a dough. The chapattis are rolled out from this dough and cooked on a tawa.

Mohan maas/Safed maas: It is a rich preparation of mutton with lots of cream, spices and milk usually taken with Roti.

Mongidi chawal: It is prepared with rice and fried lentil dumplings known as mongodis. It is preparing by putting whole hot spices in the ghee followed by some sliced onions, ginger juliennes, and other spices. The soaked rice is added and cooked along with fried mongodis.

Panchkuta: This is a quintessential curry made up of five ingredients found widely across the Thar Desert. It has a long shelf life after being cooked and is traditionally eaten with pooris/rotis. The five ingredients of panchkuta are sangri, ker, Kumat (seeds from the pod of a deciduous tree), gunda (a kind of wild berry) and dry red chillies.

Papad ki sabzi: Papad Ki Sabzi is a popular Rajasthani dish that is prepared by sautéing the fried papads in gravy made of curd and tomatoes. It can be enjoyed with chapattis, Missi Roti, bajra roti, parantha, or rice.

Pathorey: These are fritters made by combining gram flour, curd, turmeric, chilli powder, mustard seeds, and ghee. They can be eaten as snacks or even stewed in a kadhi to make pathorey ki kadhi.

Pittod: It is synonymous with the word bliss, as far as edibility is concerned. A batter of gram flour is cooked in sizzling oil with mustard seeds and onion slices. This cooked paste is then spread evenly on a thaal for cooling down. Once the paste cools down enough to get the consistency of a jelly, it is cut in diagonal stripes. These diamond shaped pieces are then used in making a finger-licking curry.

Pyaaz kachori: Pyaaz kachori, a popular spicy snack from in and around Jodhpur has not only found place in almost every snacks shop of Rajasthan but has also gained much popularity in other north Indian regions. It is a deep fried puffy pastry stuffed with spicy onion that is usually relished with sweet and sour imli (tamarind) ki chutney.

Raabori: The hot red-chilli-and-garlic chutney (a type of tangy Indian sauce),

Raab: This is a thick broth made from millet (bajra) flour and buttermilk, which is heated and fermented. Bajra flour and buttermilk are put in an earthen pot and mixed to make a thick sauce. This is then left to simmer over a low flame for several hours until fully cooked. It is then eaten, usually as a soup. A variant is 'makki ki raab', or corn raab, in which boiled corn kernels are added.

Rabodi: It is all-time favorite home-made food for Rajasthanis, resembling regular small-sized papads. They are made of maize flour and buttermilk and raw dried and can be preserved for a couple of years making it a perfect survival food for the drought-prone areas of Rajasthan.

Rabri: Milk is boiled on a low flame for a long time till it becomes dense. Sugar, spices and nuts are boiled into the thickened milk until the whole liquid changes colour and turn pinkish brown. It is then chilled and served in earthen cups as dessert.

Rotlas: A thick roti made of jawar, bajra, makai on an upside down earthen pot is a dish commonly used by the kalbelias one of the most common tribals

Seera: It is sweet made of wheat flour in ghee and and roasted in a kadhai.

Tikkad: Tikkad are special Rajasthani flat breads made of flour of wheat and bengal gram, semolina, fennel seeds and milk. These Tikkads can either be fried or roasted, depending on the desired output. Though Tikkad tastes toothsome with any spicy savoury dish, it is mostly served with aloo-pyaaz ki sabzi in Rajasthan.

CHAPTER TWELVE

Rajasthani Regional Delicacies

Each region of Rajasthan has its own special food item that is identified with the town or city.

- **Jaipur** the capital city of Rajasthan has its specialty of Mishri Mawa, Kalakand and Ghevar. The *Kachchwaaha* family of Jaipur in Rajasthan is the originator of the delicacy called *Safed Maas*. The preparation is white in colour and is prepared from white mutton. The curry is prepared from cashew nuts, almonds, fresh coconut kernel paste, white pepper and poppy seeds.

- **Bikaner** has its savouries, especially bhujiya, which has accounted for its fame, and the quality of its papads and badi remains unrivalled. In sweets rasogollas are mouthwatering. The lean mutton of the desert goats of this region too is considered the most favourable.

- In **Bharatpur**, milk sweets, rarely commercially available, occupy a niche by themselves. A Rajasthani delicacy, linked with the monsoon festival of Teej, is called *ghevar*, consisting of round cakes of white flour over which sweetened syrup is poured. Today, variations include lacings with cream and khoya, making it a delightful concoction.

- Muslim food has also occupied a place in the overall cuisine of Rajasthan, no t just in pockets such as **Tonk and Loharu**, but also in *Jaipur*, Rajasthan.
- The region of Mewar or **Udaipur** in Rajasthan is believed to have come up the form of barbecue called *Sooley and Dil Jani*.
- The region of **Jodhpur** in Rajasthan is famous for Makhaniya Lassi, Kachoris, hot green masala chilies and Laddoos.
- The region of **Jaisalmer** in Rajasthan is famous for Laddoos.
- **Pushkar** is famous for its variety of Malpua.
- **Ajmer** in Rajasthan is famous for *Sohan Halwa*.
- Doodhiya Kheech is a decadent wheat and milk pudding specialty of Udaipur.
- **Alwar** is well known for Mawa, Kalakand and hot Jalebies are available in most town and cities of Rajasthan.
- Scarcity of water, fresh green vegetables have all had their effect on the cooking. In the desert belt of Jaisalmer, Barmer *and* Bikaner, cooks use the minimum of water and prefer, instead, to use more milk, buttermilk and clarified butter

CHAPTER THIRTEEN

Festivals and Celebrations of Rajasthan

While some festivals are traditional & religious, others are purely cultural fairs. Have a look at the below list of festivals of Rajasthan.

Teej – Worship of Goddess Teej:

Teej is celebrated during the monsoon season, between July and August. On this occasion, married women seek the blessings of Lord Shiva and Parvati for a happy marital life. The festival in Rajasthan is a precursor to the monsoon. It welcomes the rains given that Rajasthan's many areas are desert regions.

Teej Festival is also the festival of swings. Hung from trees, the swings are elaborately decorated, especially with flowers. Women are dressed in traditional costumes that are mostly green in color. During this time, married women sing and dance and invoke the blessings of the almighty and it is one of the best fairs and festivals of Rajasthan.

These married women are also given gifts from their parents. Usually, they are items that women use to beautify themselves such as henna, vermillion, bangles, and bindi. Gifts include sweets as well with Ghevar, a special type of Rajasthani sweet being the most popular.

Lahariya, a multicolored sari is another thing that is received by these women with glee. On this day of the festival, married women wear the sari and beautify themselves. Fairs and processions are conducted in honor of Goddess Teej – the incarnation of Parvati.

Month of Celebration : July-August

Timings : All day and Night

Duration of Celebration: One to two days

Celebrated : In and around Jaipur

Activities : During this auspicious celebration, a procession is held from the Tripoli Gate to Chaugan Stadium. Elephants, horses and camels are decorated at their best and the fleet lead the procession of Goddess Teej, accompanied by folk music and songs.

International Kite Festival – A Vibrant Festival of Rajasthan:

One of the most vibrant and popular festivals of Rajasthan, The International Kite Festival is celebrated around Makar Sankranti every year. Locals, as well as tourists, fly kites of various shapes & colours and relish local delicacies and sweets available everywhere.

Where: Jaipur and Jodhpur

Key attractions: Kite War, fireworks, illuminated kites, and sweets like Ghevar, Til-paati, Gajak, & kheer

Dates for International Kite Festival 2022: 14th January

Jaipur Literature Festival – The Greatest Literary Show On Earth:

This is aptly illustrated as the greatest literary show on Earth, showcasing works of amateur as well as most reputed writers. From Nobel Laureates & Man Booker Prize Winners to budding writers, every literature enthusiast visits Diggi Palace for this literature fiesta. This is one of the most famous festivals of Rajasthan and offers a lovely scope for spectators from Rajasthan and other parts of the world to gain knowledge from and share ideas with contemporary legendary stalwarts.

Where: Jaipur

Key attractions: Book releases, seminars, debates, chat shows, and poetry sessions

Dates for JLF 2022: 28rd January – 1st February

Elephant Fair – The Traditional Festival of Rajasthan:

The Elephant Festival is held every year during February and March at Jaipur and is among the prominent fairs and festivals of Jaipur. As is evident, elephants are the center of attention in the festival who are cleaned thoroughly, painted with bright colors, and draped in jewelry.

Large anklets are placed on their gigantic feet. Their torsos are decorated with motifs and ornamental rugs are placed on their backs.

The ears of these gigantic pachyderms are fitted with earrings. Their tusks are fitted with circular bracelets and rings made of silver. Mahouts manning these elephants are dressed to detail as well.

They appear royal and princely in their brocade jackets and brightly textured turbans. All of this does not go wasted given that there is a prize for the best dressed elephant and mahout.

This festivals in Rajsthan presents an opportunity to see grandly decorated pachyderms. Organized by the Rajasthan Tourism, the festival is held in the Jaipur Polo grounds. These regal creatures are dressed and paraded across the length and breadth of the grounds.

Elephants have always commanded a special place in the Indian society. Lord Ganesha, a popular Indian god is a deity with an elephant head. It is chiefly due to the popularity of Lord Ganesha that elephants have become popular in the fairs of Rajasthan.

Month of Celebration : February/March

Timings : All day

Duration of Celebration: One day

Celebrated : In and around Jaipur

Activities : One of the most joyous celebrations in Rajasthan, during the Elephant Festival, a number of competitions is organised. Elephant race, polo, tug of war and elephant decoration are the major attractions. Colour and music are the important parts of this festivity.

Winter Festival – Explore Various Forms of Arts

The Winter Festival was started to provide people a reason to take a break from their monotonous lives. This festival is yet another colorful and energetic festival of Rajasthan. Held over a period of three days, the festival is characterized by fun and frolic activities.

Set in one of the most picturesque locations in Rajasthan, the festival revelers may not be able to get over the enchanting beauty of Mount Abu. When visiting the fair, visitors are treated with a lot of warmth and care.

This attitude is reminiscent of the age-old culture of hospitality of Rajasthan. This combined with the joyous ambience leaves a positive impression in the mind of people.

There are numerous folk dance and musical performances held during this time. The folk singers croon classic songs that reverberate with the rich culture and history of Rajasthan. The Ghoomar and Gair singers mesmerize the audiences with their exotic dance moves and it is one of the best fairs and festivals of Rajasthan.

These are traditional folk dances and best seen in such fairs. The quality of dance performances is fabulous. A lot of effort and precision is evident in each move that the dancers make.

Cultural events are only half the story. The Winter Festival features sports events as well. There are rowing competitions and cricket matches that are held during this time. If you visit the Nakki Lake, then don't be surprised if you find a large number of lit lamps floating on the serene waters.

This is an amazing scene to watch and worth photographing a thousand times. The Winter Festival features multiple processions as well. All in all, it is one amazing festival.

Month of Celebration : March/April
Timings : All day and Night
Duration of Celebration: 3 days
Celebrated: Starts RTDC Hotel Shikhar
Activities: It is the only festival in Rajasthan, where cricket

has been introduced as a part of the celebration. During this occasion, several water sports, rowing competitions and other cultural activities are also organised.

Summer Festival – Summer Festival on The Day Of Buddha Poornima:

Mount Abu is a hill station. As a matter of fact, it is the only hill station in Rajasthan. In the month of May, this place plays host to the Summer Festival, one of the most unique amongst the fairs and festivals of Rajasthan. Held over a period of three days, the festival starts on the day of Buddha Poornima.

The fiesta starts with an elaborate ceremony that includes the singing of ballads. This is followed by a procession of bright colors and lights. Post-this, local musicians and folk dancers entertain the audiences with their performances.

There are numerous music shows that leave everyone enthralled. The Sham-e-Qawwali, an event that features some of the best Qawwali singers is held late in the day.

Close-by, the Nakki Lake hosts numerous boat races. There are horse racing events conducted as well. Organized by the Rajasthan Tourism Department, the Summer Festival attracts thousands of tourists. The highlight of the festival is the performances by the Daph and Ghoomar artists.

On the third day, the festival concludes with a bang. There are colorful fireworks and pyrotechnics that are held to mark the end of the festival. The festival is unique given its setting.

The gorgeous landscape of Mount Abu makes the event enchanting and the combination of lakes and verdant hills makes for a delightful festival experience.

Month of Celebration : Month of May on Budh Poornima

Timings : All day and Night

Duration of Celebration : 3 days

Celebrated : Starts RTDC Hotel Shikhar

Activities : This festival closes on a delightful note. Skating race, CRPF Band Show, skater's show, boat race, tug of war, paniharimatka race and deepdan are some of the events that are organised on the second and third day of this fair.

Brij Holi – The Worship of Lord Krishna:

Celebrated few days before Holi, this special Brij Holi is celebrated with the worship of Lord Krishna, dance, music, and splashing of colors. This is one of the most famous fairs and festivals of Rajasthan. Local people take a dip in the ghats of Banganga River before offering prayer to the Radha Krishna Temple.

Where: Bharatpur

Key attractions: Enactment of Raslila

Dates for Brij Holi 2022: 18th March

Urs Festival – Celebrated At The Holy Tomb of Sufi Saint Khwaja Moinuddin Chisti:

The Urs festival is celebrated at the holy tomb of Sufi Saint Khwaja Moinuddin Chisti, memorializing his emblematic unification with Allah (God). Observed every year from 1st to 6th day of Rajab (7th Islamic month), this is one of the religious festivals of Rajasthan and attracts followers from all over the world. Here, the tomb is cleaned with rosewater & draped with an embroidered silk cloth.

This is followed by prayers and offerings.

Where: Ajmer

Key attractions: Sajjada Nashin white flag hoisting, Qawwalis, and Mehfil sessions.

Date for Urs 2022: 18th February

Pushkar Camel Fair – A Camel Trade Fair:

This is one of the most traditional festivals in Rajasthan, where thousands and thousands of camels gather for trading. These ones of its kind carnivals are celebrated with music, dance and magic show, acrobats, snake charmers and carousel rides.

Where: Pushkar

Key attractions: Parade & beauty contests of well-decorated camels, hot-air balloon ride, moustache competition, and handicraft bazaar

Dates for Pushkar Camel Fair 2022: 11th November – 22nd November

Rajasthan International Folk Festival – A Celebration of Traditional Folk Music And Arts:

The Jodhpur RIFF is an annual festival that has been organized in Jodhpur since 2007. It aims to promote traditional folk music and arts. It is held every year on the Sharad Purnima – the brightest full moon of the year – at the Mehrangarh Fort in Jodhpur.

Where: Mehrangarh Fort, Jodhpur

Key attractions: Folk music & dance, jazz night, early morning ragas, and various interactive sessions

Dates for Shree Festival 2022: 29th October – 2nd

November

Kolayat Fair – The Kapil Muni Fair:

Popularly known as the Kapil Muni Fair, this mesmerising carnival is one of the most popular festivals in Rajasthan. During this event, all the 52 ghats are beautifully decorated. People offer sweetmeats, milk pudding, and sugar drops to the idols of the deity. Devotees also take dip in the holy Kolayat Lake.

Where: Kolayat, Bikaner

Key attractions: Floating of oil lamps by the believers and cattle trading

Mewar Festival – The World's 2nd Living Heritage Festival:

Mewar Festival welcomes the spring season. Observed and celebrated throughout Rajasthan, it is treated with a lot of zest and camaraderie.

Udaipur is the epicenter of this festival as Mewar rulers governed the state from Udaipur. So, this is the place to be to get the best experience this festival. During this time, the city of Udaipur wears a different look.

The whole city seems to be drenched in the colors of the fiesta. This is evident from how the shops and establishments in Udaipur decorate their external surroundings.

Bright lights and decorative art are displayed in front of commercial establishments.

The Mewar Festival is yet another festival in Rajasthan that has significance for women. During this time, women dress in their finest attire and look their best. One of the highlights here is the dressing up of Isar, who is an incarnation of Lord Shiva.

Gangaur (Parvati) is dressed up as well. These idols are then carried through the streets in a grand procession. The destination of the procession is towards the Gangaur Ghat that is located at Pichola Lake.

The idols are placed in boats and immersed into the lake. After this, people dance and celebrate. Many cultural events are held along with fireworks.

Month of Celebration : March/April

Timings : All day and Night

Duration of Celebration: One to two days

Celebrated : In and around Udaipur

Activities : During this festival, women beautify themselves in the best possible way. They wrap themselves in colourful saris and adorn traditional jewellery. Festivity can be seen all across Udaipur

Marwar Festival, Jodhpur:

There are several Jodhpur festivals. But the most popular among them is the Marwar Festival. This festival is held in memory of the heroes of the state. Originally known as the Maand Festival, the Marwar Festival is held during September to October. Celebrated over two days, the highlight of the festival is the folk music and dance performances.

The best of folk dancers and musicians assemble to provide great performances that retain their legacies. These are the very performances that were enacted out in front of kings centuries ago. The folk music and songs remind the audience of the days of yore...the battles that were fought, the sacrifices that were made and the people who became martyrs and it is among the best fairs and festivals of Rajasthan.

Another highlight of the Marwar Festival is the Camel Tatoo show. This along with the polo event are the sport events in the festival. The Mehrangarh fort and Umaid Bhawan Palace are the main venues for this and it is one of the best festivals of Rajasthan.

Both these forts are symbolic of the might and valor that existed during the reign of the Rajputs and the **fairs of Rajasthan**. The music and dance performances are specific to the Marwar region in Rajasthan. The folk dancers display an energetic performance.

The singers sing in memory of slain heroes. It is a significant event given that the people here take pride in their ancestry as warriors.

Month of Celebration : September-October

Timings : All day.

Duration of Celebration : Two days

Celebrated : In and around Jodhpur

Activities : Celebrated in the memories of the valorous warriors of Rajasthan, it is held at the UmaidBhavan Palace, Mehrangarh and Mandore. Camel polo and tattoo show are the main attractions of this festival.

Kumbhalgarh Festival – The Cultural Feast:

Kumbhalgarh Festival is known for its vibrant musical shows, extravagant dance recitals by local artists, and spectacular firework displays. This **famous festival of Rajasthan** is held with the Kumbhalgarh Fort in the backdrop. The cultural feast is truly a paradise for art and culture enthusiasts.

Where: Kumbhalgarh, Udaipur
Key attractions: Mehendi and turban tying contests
Dates for Kumbhalgarh Festival 2022: 3rd December

Bundi Festival – Three Day-Long Cultural Extravaganza:

Bundi Utsav is a 3-day-long cultural extravaganza. The marvellous carnival organized by RTDC includes a majestic procession. Ethnic sports, folk dance performances, cultural events, and competitions are the primary highlights of the festival.

Where: Bundi
Key attractions: Competitions of bridal makeup, mustache, turban tying, kabaddi, horse riding, and camel race

Matsya Festival – Discover Adventurous Sports During Festival:

Another **famous festival of Rajasthan,** the Matsya Festival is a two-day festival celebrated in the month of November in Alwar. It is attended by plenty of natives and foreign tourists.

Where: Alwar
Key attractions: Hot air ballooning, parasailing, zorbing, yoga, and stunning adventure-filled army exhibition
Date for Matsya Festival 2022: 15th April

Desert Festival – The Expansive Thar Desert:

Held in the month of February, the city of Jaisalmer is colored with the hues of festivity. This is the time when the Desert Festival is held. This festival is about camel races, competitions involving turban typing, and a host of cultural extravaganzas.

It is here that the best mustached man is chosen! Everything is unique and exotic about the Desert Festival of Jaisalmer. You celebrate the festivities amidst the vast and sun-burnt sands of the Thar Desert. You sit on a sea of golden sand as you enjoy the cultural music and dance and merry making under the moonlit sky.]

This is a three day event and which was initially started for foreign tourists. In these three days, the many facets and the cultural backdrop of Rajasthan is squeezed into the itinerary. Rajasthani folk singers and dancers enthrall the audience with their pure art form.

On the dance floor, one can find the very best of dancers and singers showcasing their amazing talent. The most popular event is the moustache competition. Everybody gets to choose their favourite moustached man. Later, people are seen getting photographed alongside these mustached men.

The fair and fire dancers also steal the show. The final countdown to the gala events starts with the visit to the Sam Sand Dunes. Over here, festival revelers get to ride camels. Folk artists perform way into the night silhouetted by sand dunes.

Month of Celebration : February

Timings : All day and Night

Duration of Celebration : 3 Day event

Celebrated : Deserts of Jaisalmer

Activities : During this festival, the life and culture of Rajasthan is showcased in a broader aspect. The Border Security Force also takes part in 'camel tattoo' and gymnasts display their skills on camel's back; 'Camel Polo' is the major attraction of this fair.

Nagaur Cattle Fair – The Ramdeoji Cattle Fair:

As the name suggests, this annual fair is meant primarily for cattle trading. Almost 70,000 bullocks, camels, and horses are traded. The cattle are extravagantly adorned and their owners dress up with multicolored turbans and long moustaches. Along with animals, spices are traded. Jugglers, puppeteers, and storytellers are also seen here.

Where: Nagaur

Key attractions: Mirchi Bazaar (largest red chilli market of India) and sale of wooden items, iron crafts, and camel leather accessories

Dates for Cattle Fair 2022: 17th February – 20th February

Baneshwar Festival – The Tribal Festival Of Rajasthan:

Baneshwar Festival is one of the popular tribal and cultural festivals of Rajasthan. Organised in the Baneshwar temple of Dungarpur, the festival is of most significance to the Bhills tribe. The tribe comes here all the way from Gujarat, Rajasthan, and Madhya Pradesh to take a holy dip at the convergence of Mahi and Som River.

Where: Dungarpur

Key attractions: Animal shows and puppet dance

Dates for Baneshwar Festival 2022: 23th February – 27th February

Chandrabhaga Fair – A Religious Cum Cattle Fair:

This religious cum cattle fair pulls travelers, cattle herders, pilgrims, and explorers from all over the country to assemble on the banks of river Chandrabhaga for a holy dip and prayer. However, for most locals, it holds a greater significance for cattle trading.

Where: Jhalawar

Key attractions: Deep Daan, Shobha yatra, cattle fair & trading, and various competitions

Dates for Chandrabhaga Fair 2022: 7th to 9th February

Kota Adventure Festival – A Heaven For Adventure Enthusiasts:

Kota is a heaven for adventure enthusiasts from all over the world. People visit this festival to rejoice a wide range of thrilling adventure sports and also take part in rural expeditions by the banks of River Chambal. Be a part of one of this amazing **Rajasthan festivals 2020** and have a great time here in Kota.

Where: Kota

Key attractions: Parasailing, rafting, windsurfing, water skiing, kayaking, rock climbing, trekking, gliding, and fishing

Dates for Kota Adventure Festival 2022: 30th September to 17th October

Gangaur Festival – Symbolizes Togetherness Of Lord Shiva And Goddess Parvati:

The Gangaur Festival is celebrated with much aplomb across Rajasthan. The word Gangaur is a combination of two words - Gan which is a synonym for Lord Shiva and Gaur which is used to refer Goddess Parvati.

This festival is held in commemoration of Goddess Parvati. The Goddess is revered and worshipped for possessing many qualities such as marital love, courage, strength, and power. Married women worship the deity for happiness and a long married life. They pray that their husbands continue to make wealth and provide for the family.

The Gangaur festivals of Rajasthan is celebrated during March and April. This is during the month of Chaitra, which as per the Hindu calendar is the starting month. Married women observe fast and eat only once a day.

During the festival, these women wear new clothes and jewelry. They apply mehandi on their feet and decorate their palms with henna. On the seventh day of the festival, women carry earthen pots on their heads that are used as containers for gifts received from elders.

The ritual lasts for approximately ten days. On the final day the earthen pots are broken. A procession takes place during this day starting from Zanani-Deodhi in Rajasthan and concluding at Talkatora.

Month of Celebration : March/April
Timings : All day and Night
Duration of Celebration: 18 Days
Celebrated : In and around Jaipur
Activities : Women make clay idols and on the 7th day of the festival, they break the earthen pots and dispose the pieces into water. The idols are also immersed in water on this day. Ghewar, a typical Rajasthani sweet is widely enjoyed during this festival.

Mahashivratri – In The Honour Of Lord Shiva:

Mahashivratri is a Hindu festival celebrated in the honour of Lord Shiva. One of the auspicious **Rajasthan festivals 2020,** it is celebrated all over India and is a holiday in most states. There are lots of mythological beliefs associated with this festival. Lord Shiva is facilitated with flowers, honey and bel leaves and most of the women observe fast on this day.

Where: All over Rajasthan

Key attractions: Colourful decoration of Shiv temple

Dates for Mahashivratri 2022: 11 March

Ashwa Poojan – The Regal Festival of Horse Worshipping:

Ashwa Poojan is the regal festival of worshipping the horse organized in Udaipur on the 9th day of Navratri. This is the most **famous festival of Rajasthan** that acknowledges relationship between honour and horse. The horse is worshipped by the eldest member of the house followed by a delicious Rajasthani cuisine treat.

Where: Udaipur

Key attractions: Worshipping the Horse

Dates for Ashwa Poojan 2022: 17th November

Kabir Yatra – The Folk Music Of Rajasthan:

Kabir Yatra is one of a kind festival that celebrates the folk music of Rajasthan. It is a travelling music festival all over Rajasthan that is great for travellers who would like to enjoy the state's folk music. What makes the festival unique is that the 6 days journey in and around Bikaner acts as a stage for the local musicians to express their skills and talents.

Where: Bikaner
Key attractions: Folk music of Rajasthan

Ramdevra Fair – Celebrated In The Memory Of Baba Ram Dev:

Ramdevra Fair is a significant fair held in memory of Baba Ram Dev in a small village in Jaisalmer. Every year, it attracts devotees to Ramdevji's temple, where his samadhi exists too. People from different religions come to the temple and offer prayers. What makes the fair significant is that people from different walks of life come and unite together to be a part of the celebrations.

Where: Jaisalmer
Key attractions: Melodious bhajans and kirtan
Dates for Ramdevra Fair 2022: 16th September

Gogaji Fair, Hanumangarh:

Gogaji Fair takes place to commemorate the hero Goga Veer (also known as Jahar Peer) among Hindus and Muslims. The place of the fair is Goga Medi which is around three hundred and sixty kilometers from Jaipur.

Gogaji's memorial or Samadhi is at this place. His Samadhi houses his idol that is seen sitting on a blue horse and close-by is a statue of a coiled snake.

The Kayam Khani Muslims have given Gogaji the stature of a saint. It is believed that anyone suffering from snakebite can get cured if they prayed to him. The influence of this revered man is such that a Than is dedicated to him in every Rajasthani village.

Gogaji has devotees across many parts of North India and not just Rajasthan. Devotees come from Gujarat,

Maharashtra, and Madhya Pradesh. Many people are repeat visitors. They re-visit the Samadhi to express their gratitude for a granted wish.

The annual fair is held in the month of August for a duration of three days. Apart from worshiping the idol with cupped hands, rubbing incense at his idol is another form of worship. Devotees also offer coconuts, cash, and sugar sweetmeats at his tomb and it is one of the best fairs in Rajasthan.

Outside the Samadhi, Nath priests carry whips called as Chabuks. These whips are considered to bring luck hence are worshipped by the devotees.

Month of Celebration : Month of Bhadrapada during the Gogaji fair

Timings : All day

Duration of Celebration : 3 days

Celebrated : Gogameri

Activities : During this fair, the believers and followers of Gogaji wrap up live snakes around their necks and lie near the temple. According to them,Gogaji protects them from the snakes and its bite. The life and stories of the deity is also recited on this eve.

Karni Mata Fair, Bikaner:

This fair is held in reverence of Karni Mata. This deity is said to be one of the main goddesses of the rulers of Bikaner several centuries ago. The venue of the fair is at the temple of the goddess. Made of stone and marble, this temple is ruggedly built yet oozes divine elegance.

Of the fairs and festivals of Rajasthan, this is one fair that is held two times in a year. The first fair is the larger one of the two and is held between March and April. The second fair is held between September and October. People belonging to the Rajput caste bring their children here to get their first haircuts. On this occasion, children along with their parents seek the blessings of Karni Mata.

One of the greatest sights during the fair is the presence of a huge number of brown rats. These rats inhabit the temple and are considered holy. The more stunning part is that they are harmless. If anyone sees a white rat amongst the brown rat, it is considered to be an auspicious sign.

The temple is called the Karni Mata temple. Located at Deshnok, it is open to the public as early as 4 AM. Inside the temple is a shrine that houses the idol of the goddess that is only 75 cms.

Month of Celebration : March-April and September-October

Timings : All day and Night

Duration of Celebration : One to two days

Celebrated : In and around Bikaner

Activities : Devotees from different parts of Rajasthan visit the Karni Mata Temple and seek her blessings during this fair. The children usually get their first hair cut on this eve and devotes offer gold or silver upon the fulfilment of their wishes.

CHAPTER FOURTEEN

Traditional Rajasthani Recipes

Saadi Baati

Ingredients:

- 300 gm - Wheat flour
- 100 gm - Semolina
- Ghee - as per requirement
- 1 teaspoon - Salt
- ½ litre – Water

Method:

- Mix salt, 6 tbsp. ghee, flour and semolina and knead into stiff dough with a little water. Cover with a wet cloth and set aside for half an hour.
- Break the dough into about 10 pieces. Flatten the dough and press the centre with your thumb.
- Place the baati in half litre of boiling water for 10 minutes and lift out onto paper towels.
- Roast the baati in an oven (grill) until golden brown.

- Dip each baati in hot ghee and serve with dal, churma, gatta curry and garlic chutney for a real Rajasthani feast.

Padampuri Murg

Ingredients:

- 750 gm chicken
- One pod of garlic
- ½ tsp coriander seeds
- ½ tsp ginger-finely chopped
- 2 Tbspgarlic paste
- 7 small onions-finely chopped
- 6 whole red chillies
- 5 cloves
- ½ tsp aniseed
- 2 sticks of cinnamon
- 100 gm khoya
- 250 gm yogurt
- 2 cooking spoons of clarified butter (Ghee)
- Salt according to taste

Method:

- Mix all the ingredients except for the chicken, cloves, cardamom and the cinnamon with the yogurt and keep ready.
- Heat the clarified butter and add the cloves, cardamom and cinnamon.
- Add all the ingredients except for the chicken and stir till the masalas is done.
- Add the chicken and cook till its done.

- Served garnished with chopped coriander leaves.

Makki Doodhi Ra Moothiya

Ingredients:

- 2 Tbsp vegetable oil
- ¼ Tbsp cumin seeds
- 1 stem of cinnamon
- 3 whole black pepper pinch of mace / jaivitri
- 2 pieces of cardamom
- 3 pieces of clove
- 1 cassia Leaf
- 2 finely chopped onions
- 2 Tbsp ginger garlic paste
- ¼ Tbsp coriander powder
- ¼ Tbsp red chilli powder pinch of turmeric powder
- 50 gm yoghurt
- ¼ Tbsp garam masala
- ¼ Tbsp fenugreek seeds, coriander leaves, fried whole red chillies and juliennes of ginger
- Salt to taste

Method:

- Mix corn flour with corn seed, bottle legour, oil, salt, cumin seeds, fennel, finely chopped coriander leaves, green chillies, bishops weed, finely crushed coriander seeds and water, to make a dough.
- Take the dough in your hand and roll out a few dumplings. Boil them in water.
- Now deep-fry them in vegetable oil for about 2 minutes.

- Cut the fried moothiya into tiny pieces and soak them in water till they become soft.

For the Gravy-

- Heat oil in pan and add cumin seeds. Cook them till they start crackling.
- Now add cinnamon, whole black pepper, mace, cardamom, clove, cassia leaf, onions and
- Ginger garlic paste. Saute the onions till they become translucent.
- Then add coriander powder, red chilli powder, and turmeric powder. Add salt to this and mix well.
- Add the curd to the preparation and cook for a few minutes.
- Add the water, garam masala and fenugreek seeds. Cook for 10 minutes.
- Mix the prepared moothiya and gravy together.
- Makki doodhi ra moothiya is ready to eat Garnish with coriander leafs, fried whole red chillies
- Add juliennes of ginger. Serve hot with rice.

Dal Dhokli

Ingredients:

- 3 cups maize flour (makki ka atta, yellow sweet corn flour)
- ½ cup peas
- 1 cup methi (fenugreek leaves) , finely chopped
- ½ cup cilantro , finely chopped
- 2 ½ tbsp oil

- ½ tsp baking soda
- 1 tsp coriander seeds , crushed
- 1 ½ tsp red chilli powder
- ½ tsp turmeric powder
- ½ tsp garam masala
- 1 tsp ginger , crushed
- 1 tsp green chilies , finely chopped
- Salt to taste
- Warm water , for dough
- 3 tbsp ghee

Method:

- In a bowl put maize flour, salt, red chili powder, coriander powder, turmeric powder, garam masala and oil. Mix everything together.
- Now add baking soda, peas, cilantro leaves, and fenugreek (methi) leaves to the flour mixture. Mix it well.
- Gradually add water to make a soft dough that will roughly hold its shape.
- Form the dough into round discs about 2-3 inches in diameter. Flatten them a bit and then using your fingers, press down in the middle to create a small indent, that will ensure even cooking and serve and a place to add ghee later.
- Steam them for 20 minutes in a greased dish. It can be done in a bamboo steamer, stainless steel steamer, or idli stand. For the first five minutes do it on high heat. After that make it medium heat for 10-15 mins. For the very last minute, make the flame higher and then remove if from the stove.

- Once the dhoklas are done, pour some ghee on top. It is important to use ghee as it enhances the flavor and will keep them moist.

Bajre Ki Roti

Ingredients:

- 2 cup bajra atta / pearl millet flour / sajje hittu
- ½ tsp salt
- Hot water - to knead
- Wheat flour - for dusting

Method:

- Firstly, in a large mixing bowl take 2 cup bajra atta, ½ tsp salt and mix well.
- Add ½ of hot water and start to knead.
- Knead to the soft dough for at least 10 minutes.
- Add water as required and knead well as there is no gluten in the dough.
- Pinch a small ball sized dough and knead again.
- Dust with wheat flour and pat gently. You can alternatively use a rolling pin to roll as done for paratha.
- Pat with both the hands until the roti turns as thin as possible. If the roti breaks, it means it needs more kneading.
- Dust off excess flour and put over hot tawa.
- Now spread water over the roti with help of hand or wet cloth removing excess dough.
- Wait until the water evaporates then flip it to the other side.

- Press gently and cook all the sides.
- Finally, serve bajra roti / sajje rotti with jaggery or curry.

Ghevar

Ingredients:

- 1 ½ cup all purpose flour
- 2 pieces ice cubes
- ¼ cup milk
- ½ cup ghee
- ½ cup ghee
- 2 ½ cup water
- 1/8 tea-spoon edible food color
- 1 cup sugar
- For Toppings
- ½ tea-spoon powdered green cardamom
- 1 strand saffron
- ½ table-spoon chopped almonds
- 6 inches silver film

Method:
Prepare the sugar syrup for Ghevar –

- This traditional recipe needs no introduction. Ghevar is an easy-to-make recipe and can be prepared with some easily available ingredients. To begin with you need to prepare the sugar syrup of one string consistency. Then, take a large wide bowl and add solidified ghee in it. Take one ice cube at a time and rub the ghee vigorously. Take more ice cubes as required, till the ghee becomes very white in colour.

Prepare the Ghevar batter –

- Then add milk, flour and one cup water. Mix these ingredients to make a smooth batter. Dissolve colour in some water and add to the batter. Add more water as required. The consistency of the batter should be fairly thin in texture.

Cook the Ghevar –

- Then take an aluminium or steel cylindrical container. Make sure that its height is at least 12″ and diameter is of 5-6″. Fill half of the container with ghee. Heat it and once the ghee is hot enough, then take a 50 ml, glassful of the batter. Pour in centre of ghee, slowly in one continuous thread like stream. Allow the foam to settle.

Dip the Ghevar in sugar syrup –

- Pour one more glassful in hole formed in centre. When the foam settles again, loosen the Ghevar with an iron skewer inserted in hole. Lift carefully, at a slant and place on wire mesh to drain. Keep hot syrup in a wide flat-bottomed container to fit in the Ghevar. Then, dip the Ghevar in it and remove it to drain out the excess syrup. Then, keep aside on a mesh, this will take out the extra syrup.

Cool the Ghevar and garnish with dry fruits –

- Alternatively, pour some syrup evenly all over, keeping Ghevar in a mesh placed over a container. Let it cool and settle down, then top it with silver foil. Splash a few drops of saffron milk, sprinkle some chopped dry fruits and a few pinches of cardamom powder. Serve

Lal Maans

Ingredients:

- 1 kg lamb
- 5 teaspoon red chilli powder
- 3 sliced onion
- salt as required
- 1 tablespoon garlic paste
- 2 bay leaf
- 1 cinnamon stick
- ½ cup ghee
- 3 teaspoon coriander powder
- 1 cup yoghurt (curd)
- 1 teaspoon powdered turmeric
- 2 teaspoon garam masala powder
- 4 green cardamom
- For Garnishing: 2 tablespoon chopped coriander leaves

Method:

- In a deep bottomed pan add ghee. Once hot, add cinnamon sticks, cardamom and bay leaves. Sauté for 3-5 minutes.
- Now, add the washed mutton pieces, onions, ginger-garlic paste, yogurt, turmeric and salt. Cook covered on

a low flame till the mutton pieces turn soft.

- Add the powdered spices (except garam masala) and cook till oil starts separating from the meat.
- Now, add one cup water, garam masala and again simmer for 5-7 minutes.
- Serve hot with streamed rice or paratha.

Gatte Ki Sabji

Ingredients:

- For gatte / gram flour dumplings:
- 1 cup besan / gram flour
- ½ tsp coriander seeds, crushed
- ¼ tsp ajwain / carom seeds
- ¼ tsp turmeric
- ¼ tsp kashmiri red chilli powder
- pinch hing / asafoetida
- ¼ tsp salt
- 2 tbspghee / clarified butter
- 2 tbspcurd / yogurt
- 2 tbspwater
- For sabzi:
- 2 tbspoil
- 1 tsp cumin / jeera
- 1 tsp kasuri methi / dry fenugreek leaves
- 1 bay leaf / tej patta
- ½ tsp fennel / saunf
- 1 pinch hing / asafoetida
- 1 onion, finely chopped
- 1 tsp ginger garlic paste
- ¼ tsp turmeric

- 1 tsp kashmiri red chilli powder
- ½ tsp coriander powder
- ¼ tsp cumin powder / jeera powder
- 1 cup curd / yogurt, whisk
- ½ tsp salt
- ¼ tsp garam masala
- 2 tbsp coriander, finely chopped

Method:

- In a large kadai heat 2 tbspoil and saute spices.
- Add 1 onion, 1 tsp ginger garlic paste and saute to golden brown.
- Keeping the flame on low, add spices and saute well.
- Furthermore, add 1 cup water and 1 cup curd. Stir continuously until the mixture comes to a boil.
- Now add prepare gatte (gram flour dumplings) and ½ tsp salt. Mix well.
- Cover and boil for 5 minutes.
- Additionally, add ¼ tsp garam masala and 2 tbspcoriander. Mix well.
- Finally, serve gatte ki sabji with roti, phulka or naan.

Aamras Ki Kadhi

Ingredients:

- Mango Puree – ½ cup ripe or pulpy mango + ½ cup raw green mango
- Curd – ¾ cup, mixed and whisked with ¾ cup water
- Turmeric Powder – a pinch
- Red Chilli Powder – a pinch

- Salt as per taste
- Oil – 1 tsp
- Cumin Seeds – ¼ tsp
- Fenugreek Seeds – a pinch
- Mustard Seeds – ¼ tsp
- Curry Leaves – few
- Asafoetida Powder – a small pinch
- Green Chillies – 2, small, split
- Boondi – 2 tblsp
- For tempering:
- Oil – ½ tsp
- Ginger – 1 tsp, julienned
- Dry Red Chillies – 1, broken
- Coriander Leaves 1 tsp
- Boondi – 1 tsp

Method:

- Mix the mango puree, curd, turmeric powder and red chilli powder in a bowl.
- Mix well until blended. Keep aside.
- Heat oil in pan. Add the curry powder, asafoetida powder, gren chillies, mustard seeds, fenugreek seeds and cumin seeds.
- Fry for a minute or two.
- Reduce flame and add the mango puree mixture.
- Keep stirring regularly and sprinkle salt.
- Cook for 15 minutes on low flame and add the boondi.
- Simmer for a few minutes till cooked and oil floats to the surface.
- Transfer to a serving bowl.
- Heat oil for tempering in a frying pan.

- Fry the tempering ingredients for a minute and pour into the kadhi.
- Serve hot.

Jaisalmeri Chane

Ingredients:

- Black Bengal Gram soaked overnight and boiled with salt 2 cups
- Yogurt 1½ cups
- Gram flour (besan) 4 tablespoon
- Red chilli powder 2 tablespoon
- Garam masala powder 2 tablespoon
- Turmeric powder ½ teaspoon
- Coriander powder 1 tablespoon
- Asafoetida A large pi
- Ghee 2 tablespoon
- Green chillies finely chopped 2
- Salt to taste
- Cumin seeds 1 teaspoon
- Bengal gram stock 1 cup

Method:

- Put yogurt, gram flour, 1 tsp red chilli powder, 1 tsp garam masala powder, turmeric powder, coriander powder and ¼ tsp asafoetida in a bowl and whisk well.
- Heat ghee in a non-stick pan.
- Crush half the Bengal gram lightly with a rolling pin.
- Add large pinch asafoetida and green chillies to the pan and sauté. Add remaining whole Bengal gram and

crushed Bengal gram and mix well.

- Add remaining red chilli powder, garam masala powder and salt and mix well. Add cumin seeds, mix and sauté for 2-3 minutes.
- Add 2 cups water to yogurt mixture and whisk well. Add yogurt mixture to the pan, mix and cook till gravy thickens.
- Add Bengal gram stock, mix and bring it to boil.
- Transfer into a serving bowl and serve hot.

Khoba Roti

Ingredients:

- Wheat flour - 1 cup (150 grams)
- Salt - ¼ tsp
- Cumin seed - ¼ tsp
- Ghee - 2 tbsp

Method:

- Take flour is a big bowl. Add salt, cumin seeds and 2 tsp ghee in flour and mix well. Now add little water at a time and knead bit hard dough than required for making regular roti. Cover the kneaded dough and keep aside for 20 minutes to set.

- After 20 minutes, grease your hands with some oil and knead the dough until smooth. Make a round dough ball. Place the dough ball on rolling plate and roll into ½ cm thick roti.

- For roasting roti, preheat tawa. Place the roti on heated tawa and cook on medium flame. When roti turns brown from beneath, flip the side. Make small peaks with help of your thumb and finger on the roasted side of your roti. Make peaks on the entire roti. Keep the flame to minimum. Roast until roti gets brown spots on the other side. Now flip the roti and cook from side with peaks for another 2 minutes.

- Now take off roti from tawa and place it direct on flame. Roast roti on low flame until it gets brown spots on both sides. Place the roti on plate and spread 1-2 tsp ghee over it. Pour ghee in the holes over roti. It will be absorbed completely. This will enhance the flavor.

- Delicious Khoba roti is ready. Serve with dal or any other gravy dish.

Choorma Ladoo

Ingredients:

- Wheat flour1 ½ cup coarsely grounded
- Besan ¼ cup
- Rava / Sooji ¼ cup
- Oil1 ½ tbsp
- Water½ cup
- Ghee ¼ cup
- Oil2 cup for frying
- Jaggery1/3 cup
- Powdered sugar1 ½ tbsp
- Nutmeg1/8 tsp

- Poppy seeds1 tsp for garnish
- Kismis1 tbsp

Method:
<u>To Make Churma Mixture –</u>

- In a large mixing bowl take whole wheat flour (coarsely grounded), besan (chickpea flour) and sooji / rava.
- Add 1 and ½ tbspOil and ½ cup warm water.
- Combine all ingredients and knead into dough.
- Now take a portion of wheat flour dough in hand and press it by making fist. Press hard and make Muthia shapes from dough.
- Repeat the process for remaining wheat flour dough and make muthia. Keep aside.
- Now to fry the muthia heat Oil in a deep bottom frying pan. Heat on medium flame and don't let oil turn too hot.
- Deep fry the wheat flour muthia in oil for 4 to 5 minutes. Till it is completely cooked from inside and turn golden brown.
- Take out the fried muthias and drain the excess oil on kitchen towel / paper napkin. Let the muthias cool down.
- Cut the muthias into pieces and further grind them in a food processor into fine powder. Sieve through a fine siever to remove big chunks. Re-grind the remaining chunks if required.

<u>To Make Churma Ladoo –</u>

- Take a nutmeg and pound in a mortar and pestle. Add the nutmeg powder in Churma mixture.

- Optionally you can also add dry fruits like kismis.
- Now melt ghee in a pan and add Jaggery. As soon as jaggery starts floating on ghee, turn off the gas.
- Pour the melted jaggery and ghee into Churma mixture. Add powdered sugar. Again sugar is optional.
- Combine all the ingredients and make nice aromatic churma mixture.
- Now make Churma laddus from churma by pressing it in a laddu mold. You can also make ladoo by taking a portion of churma and rolling in hands and making nice spherical balls.
- Repeat the process and make ladoos from remaining mixture.
- Apply some poppy seeds (khus khus) and garnish the churma ladoo.
- Churma ladoo is ready to serve.

Part B: Gujarat

Culinary History of Gujarat

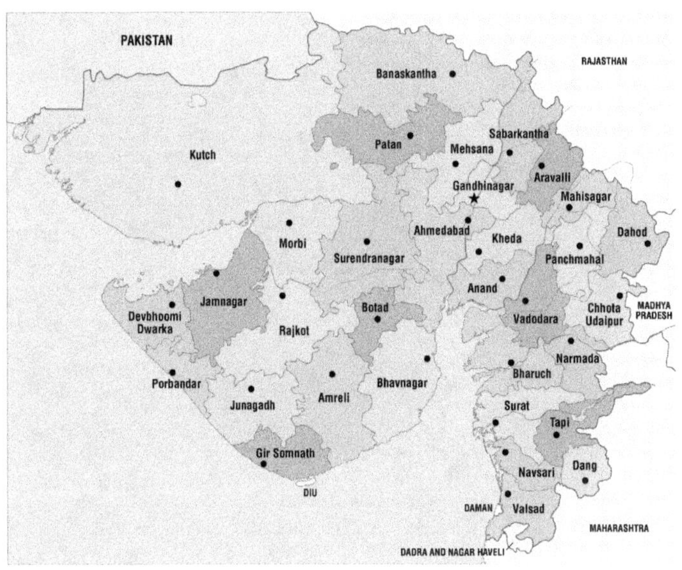

CHAPTER FIFTEEN

Geography of Gujarat

Gujarat is situated on the west coast of India. It is bounded in the west by the Arabian Sea, in the north-west by Pakistan and state border with Rajasthan in north east, Madhya Pradesh to the east and Maharashtra and union territories of Daman, Diu, Dadra and Nagar Haveli to the south. With 1290 kilometers of coast line, it boasts of having the longest coastline amongst all the coastal states of India.

<u>The state comprises of three geographical regions.</u>

- The Saurashtra or Kathiawar peninsula is essentially a hilly tract interspersed with low lying mountains. This is the occupational mainland comprising of major cities of Ahmedabad, Surat and Vadodara (Baroda), Dwarka and Rajkot .

- Kutch on the north-east is barren and rocky and is famous for the Rann (desert) of Kutch, the big Rann in the north and the little Rann in the east comprises of cities like Bhuj and Gandhidham.

- The mainland which is a fertile plain composed of alluvial soil brought down by the river Sabarmati, Mahi, Narmada and Tapti lies between the Rann of Kutch, Aravali hills and the Damanganga river.

CHAPTER SIXTEEN

A Brief History of Gujarat

Gujarat draws its name from the Gurjara which was an old Hindu clan, which inhabited the area during the Mahabharat period. Another opinion regarding Gurjars is that they belonged to Central Asia and came to India during the first century and are believed to be of Indo-Aryan origin.

The history of Gujarat encompasses the Indus Valley civilization. About 50 Harappan settlement ruins were discovered in Gujarat.

Gujarat was ruled over by a number of mighty kings, like the Mauryas, the Scythians, the Guptas, the Solankis and the Mughals. These rulers contributed to the culture of the state significantly, by building a number of monuments and popularizing other traditional practices.

The state assumed its present form in 1960, when the former Bombay state was divided between Maharashtra and Gujarat on the basis of language. It is the birth place of Mahatma Gandhi - the Father of the Nation.

The first capital of the newly found state of Gujarat was Ahmedabad but, in the year 1970, it was shifted to Gandhinagar. Today, Gujarat has transformed into one of the sought-after tourist destination of India.

CHAPTER SEVENTEEN

Climate of Gujarat

Winter (November to February) temperatures in Gujarat usually reach as high 28 degree centigrade, while lows drop to about 12 degree centigrade. Summers (March to May) are quite hot, however, with temperatures typically rising well above 38 degree centigrade during the day and dropping to almost 30 degree centigrade at night.

Gujarat is drier in the north than in the south. Rainfall is lowest in the northwestern part of the state in the Rann of Kachchh, where it may amount to less than 15 inches annually. In the central portion of the Kathiawar peninsula as well as in the northeastern region, annual rainfall typically amounts to about 40 inches. Southeastern Gujarat, where the southwest monsoon brings heavy rains between June and September, is the wettest area; annual rainfall usually approaches 80 inches along the south coastal plains.

CHAPTER EIGHTEEN

The Proud Gujarati

The people of Gujarat owe their lineage to the Gujaratis. The Gujaratis are believed to have accompanied the Huns when they migrated to India and finally got settled in Gujarat as the ancestral Gujarati tribe. The Hindus form the major part of state's population, followed by other religions. In fact, there are many castes lines - Koli, Kanbi, Brahmin, Vaishnava, Suthar, Luhar, Kadiya, Kumbhar, Rajput, Vaniya, Anavil and Lohana, which originate from the Hindu religion. Apart from the main Gujarati tribe, the state is inhabited by several ethnic tribes/groups such as Jats, Harijans, Ahirs, Rabaris, Kolis, Bhils, Mina, Naikda, Dhubla, and Macchi-Kharwa. The upper castes are Nagar Brahman and Bhatia are duly respected in the Gujrati society. Jats and Ahirs are farmers and herdsmen and cattle breeders. The Vaniyas and small proportions of Muslims, Parsis and Jains are prominent in entrepreneurship and business enterprise. Rabaris and Harijans are known for their exclusive handiworks.

Unfavorable climatic conditions, salinity of soil and water, and rocky terrain have hampered Gujarat's agricultural activities, but the sector has remained a major component of the state's economy, employing about half the workforce. Wheat, millet, rice, Bajra, Jawar (sorghum) and Pulses are the primary food crops, with rice production being concentrated in the wetter areas. Principal cash crops include cotton, oilseeds (especially groundnuts), tobacco, sugarcane and dates. Commercial dairying is also important.

Milk revolution (white revolution or 'operation flood') started and organized Milk production, processing, distribution & product marketing ('Amul' brand name is the pioneer) under Dr. Verghese (from Kerala) converted this state of cattle-wealth to dairy farmers. Spices such as cumin, fennel, fenugreek, dill seed, ajwain, mustard, sesame, garlic and coriander are also grown. Gujarat has the longest coast line and so Fisheries is a well developed economic activity.

CHAPTER NINETEEN

The Multi Dimensional Gujarati Cuisine

The cuisine of Gujarat is a multi-flavor cuisine arising from the state's cultural diversity. The flavors of Gujarat range from sweet to sour, spicy to pungent and speak loud of a mouthwatering contradiction. In other words, the culinary traditions of the state are a mixture of varied textures, colors and flavors which is heavily influenced by the geography, history, and culture of the region. Food is traditionally served on silver platters to the accompaniment of rice and a variety of wheat breads.

Typically Gujarat can be divided into four cuisines are depending on the food habits of the people:

- North Gujarat- **Ahmedabadi cuisine**
- South Gujarat- **Surti Cuisine**
- Saurashtra (Kathiawadi) - **Kathiyawadi Cuisine**
- Kutch (Kutchi)- **Kutchi Cuisine**

North Gujarat is the home of traditional Gujarati cuisine with the Gujarati Thali being very popular. It is a dish consisting of rice, dal, sprouted beans, curry, vegetables, farsan, pickles, chutney and raita. North Guajarati food is not very oily or spicy. Farsans are typically salty snacks which finds palce in almost all the meals of a Guajarati. They are of three varieties: Pathara, Khaman Dhokla, and Khandvi. Papads, chutneys and pickles accompany every meal and are preferred a lot. Ahmedabadi pulao, which is made by mixing cooked vegetables with rice, but unlike everywhere else in India, this dish has a sweet aftertaste. This region is perhaps the healthiest and conventional in its cooking with oil and spices used in minimum.

South Gujarat: It has a dominance of Surati cuisine (named after the city called Surat) which adds a lot of green chilies in their dishes. In some households, one of two chili is just bitten at in between the meal to re - establish the spiciness. Very hot region and very hot cuisine is what could be said to describe the cuisine. It is very simple and the most common dishes are perhaps the same as that of North Gujarat with just a lot of spices. Owing to plenty of rainfall lots of varieties of green vegetables and fruits are available and used. Among the popular items here at festival times are Oondhiyu and Paunk. Surti locho, a popular street food similar to dhokla served with a smattering of chutneys. These people also have a sweet tooth and one can see a lot of sweeteries and bakeries locally. Products like nankhatias, gharis and saglu-baglu methai are very popular in this region. South Guajarati eats simple food with a lot of life in it in the form of salads, chhas, fruit preserves and aam pana.

Saurashtra (Kathiawari): Since it shares a border with the neighboring state of Rajasthan, it is fair to say that Kathiyawadi cuisine is heavily influenced by Rajasthani cooking and so the cuisine is more spicy and rich and not as sweet like other Gujarati dishes. A popularity of this region is Dhebra. It is made with wheat flour, spinach, green chilies, a pint of yoghurt, salt and sugar to taste. It is eaten with a specially prepared hot and sweet mango pickle. The Kathiawari speciality spice called Methi masala (Fenugreek is dried and ground with red chilies and salt) is used in most of the dishes. In Kathiawad, it quite surprising to learn that Saurashtra in spite of its dry earth has millet, peanuts, sugarcane, wheat, and sesame. In Saurashtra during the harsh cold winter Bhakris, a type of thick rotis, made from wheat flour, garlic, onion, buttermilk and a lot of spices is made. It keeps the body warm. Phafda, an fenugreek flavoured assorted flour puri is another Kathiawari favourite. Sev tameta nu shaak is a hot curry made from tomatoes and chilli powder topped off with generous additions of sev (fried noodles made of besan). Another prominent Kathiyawadi dish is Ringna no oroh or roasted eggplant is similar to baigan kaa bhurta and is literally mouthwatering. Pulses dominate Kathiawari food and sweetmeats made of jaggary. They also eat a lot of peanut and til cookies. This region has a delicious variety of pickles called Chhundo or Athanu.

Kutchi cuisine: The dry, arid region of Kutch plays host to some individual dishes as well. A lack of leafy green vegetables limits the food choices in the region. The cuisine of this region is also very simple, but use lots of red chillies. The main dish of this region is Khichdi. It is eaten with Kadhi - a spicy gravy made of yoghurt. The Dabeli is essentially street food where pao or bread roll (ladi pao) is stuffed with a filling made with potato, a paste made with tamarind, jaggary and date, and masala. Other popular Kutchi dishes include Bajra na rotla or Indian flat bread made of pearl millet, traditionally served with either the aforementioned Ringna no oroh, or curd and garlic chutney. Khaja, a dessert reminiscent of baklava is also made here. It is prepared using refined flour, mawa, and oil, deep-fried and then dipped in sugar syrup. Khaman Dhokla, Dudhi mithiya, Khakraa, thepla, Doodhpak and Shrikhand are some of the other popular dishes.

CHAPTER TWENTY

Features of Gujarati Cuisine

"Gujaratis in general from all the four regions, namely, North Gujrat, South Gujrat, Saurashtra (Kathiawadi) and Kutch (Kutchi) eat a simple everyday meal which is daal, rice, rotli, shaak. During festive days, additional and more varieties of shaak, sweet dishes and Farsan is prepared."

Gujrati cooking does not utilize meats and also chicken and fish hardly used. Gujrati cuisine is mostly a vegetarian cuisine.

The dry Gujarati climate does not sustain the cultivation of rice. A typical Gujrati meal consists of Indian Breads (rotis) made from wheat flour, gram flour, bajra and maize. Roti itself is prepared in a number of variations from the petal soft phulkas to the bone-dry khakra.

Grinding of spices is very common as dishes seem to look and taste better with ground spices. Oil is also not used much. Both spice and oil are both kept at a minimum.

Certain ingredients like ghee, yogurt, buttermilk, coconut, groundnut, til seeds, lime juice, fenugreek, chat masala, sugar, jaggary etc. are very common in Gujarati food. Many Gujarati dishes are distinctively sweet, salty, and spicy at the same time. The use of jaggary, kokum, lime and tamarind is in plenty. It is common to add a little sugar or jaggary to some of the sabzi/shaak and daal which is believed to neutralize the slightly salty taste of the water. Tangy, salty and spicy flavors too are a part of the flavors range of a typical Gujarati cuisine which is diverse and delectable.

The cuisine makes a generous use of lemons, limes, tomatoes, salt and sugar to check dehydration especially in the summer months when temperatures hover around 45 to 50 degree centigrade.

The cuisine changes with the seasonal availability of vegetables. An assorted combination of green leafy vegetables, seasonal healthy vegetables, with a delectable collection of spices makes it very palatable and tasty.

The spices used also change depending on the season. Garam Masala and its constituent spices are used less in summer.

Regular fasting, with diets limited to milk and dried fruits, and nuts is common. Goodness of milk, yoghurt, buttermilk, coconuts, groundnuts and various other nuts make this meal rich in proteins even with the absence of meat and eggs.

Papads include the kheechara, which contains wheat, rice, and bajra flours, and is neither fried nor baked, but steamed.

Meals are mostly accompanied by chaas or homemade buttermilk and homemade pickles (Athanu or Chhundo).

Raithas are made from curd and a combination of vegetables, nuts, dried fruits and chutneys.

Pickles include the distinctive Athanu, Goondas and Chanduo with its sweet-sour flavor, tempered with cardamom and cloves.

Sweets and chaats are another most important feature of a proper full course Gujarati meal. Gajar ka halwa, besan halwa, sweet stuffed Ghari-Puri, Malpwa, Laddoos, among the sweet dishes and Papdi Chaat, Kachori Chaat, Samosa Chaat, Raj Kachori Chaat, Dhokla, are some of the most popular of Gujarati snacks.

Farsans or Side Dishes: No dish of Gujarat is complete without the Farsans or snacks. Chaats, chutneys, sauces make awesome side dishes. Other varieties are Dabeli, Locho, Bhajiya, Sev, Ragdaa, Patra, Dahi vada, Khaman dhokla, Methi na gota, Pani puri, Muthiya, Sev Khamani, Vegetable Handvo, Makai no dana, Dal Vada, Khichdo , samosa, Ganthiya, Hahdwoh, Kachori, Khakhra, Khichu etc.

There is a specific dietary rule followed using the following four combinations. For example, if Kadhi is served, then a daal or vaal will also be included. The sweet dish accompanying kadhi will likely be milk or yogurt-based, like Doodhpak or Shrikhand. In such a meal raita would not be served. Festive meals which serve daal will typically have a wheat-based sweet dish like Lapsi or Ladu as the sweet accompaniment.

Seasoning of food is thereby given great importance with mustard, fenugreek, thyme and asafoetida used both for flavour and as digestive aids. The spices used also change depending on the season. Garam Masala and its constituent spices are used less in summer.

The Parsi and Bohri Muslim community has a distinctive cuisine style in Gujrat with an identity of their own.

In modern times, some Gujaratis have become increasingly fond of very spicy and fried dishes. There are many chefs who have come up with fusions of Western and Gujarati food.

The Kharwa community developed a style of cooking that comprise of fresh as well as dried fish. Some of the seafood usually consumed includes prawns, lobster, pomfrets, crabs and khandwas, gidadas, surmai, among others.

Seasonings/Spices: Spices used in Gujarati dishes add to the dish its characteristic flavor and taste. The seasonings and spices commonly used in Gujarati cuisine are:

- Havej or Turmeric Powder
- Aamli or Tamarind
- Kesar or Saffron
- Good or Jaggary
- Kokum
- Methi or Fenugreek seeds
- Elaichi or Cardamom
- Sarson or mustard
- Jeeru or Cumin
- Kothmir or Coriander
- Hing or Asafetida
- Pudina or Mint
- Soonth or ginger powder
- Mitho limdo or curry leaves
- Lavang or Cloves
- Chaat masala

- Lilu marchu or green chili
- Lal marchu or red chili
- Garam Masala; a mix of roasted, powdered spices

Pickles and Condiments: Pickles and Condiments accompany every scrumptious meal and lip-smacking snacks in the state of Gujarat. The pickles and condiments mostly offer one with an unforgettable lip-licking experience. The major condiments include athanu, chutney, papad, raita. Chutneys are made out of ingredients like Anjeer or fig, tamarind, garlic, bananas etc. Popular pickles of Gujarat include green chili pickle, methia Keri, lemon pickle, carrot and cucumber pickle.

Sweets and Chaats: Sweets or desserts of Gujarat are truly delectable and dear to the heart of all who have a sweet tooth. The major Gujarati sweets and desserts include Malpua, Laddoos, Ghari-puri with sweet stuffings, Besan Halwa, Gajar ka halwa, Ghoogra, Kansar, Doodh pak, Basundi, Lapsi, Sukhadi, Kopra pak.

The chaats of Gujarat are no less famous. Today the chaats of Gujarat are enjoyed countrywide as popular street foods. The most common types of chaats include Kachori chaat, Raj Kachori chaat, Papdi chaat, Dhokla, Samosa chaat etc.

Breads or Rotlo: Breads or Rotlos in Gujarat are made out of ingredients like bajra, gram flour, wheat flour, Jowar etc. breads may be made out of one single flour or a combination of many flours. Unleavened thin rotlis made of wheat are a staple in every Gujarati household. Apart from these, the other types of Rotlas/rotlis include Bakhris or crispy & thin whole wheat breads, theplas; a typical griddle bread, puris fried deep in oil and many more types. Within the genre of Gujarati breads there can be delicious variations like masala puri or methi thepla.

Rice or Bhaat: Gujarati thali has rice or bhaat as one of its major ingredients. The rice of Gujarat may have several variations. It could be plain rice or could be the spiced, sweet & tangy Khatta-meetha bhaat flavored with lemon rinds. Also, you have other types of rice preparations like the aromatic Pulao, a vegetable studded rice, Khichdi; a rice-lentil soup, Biranj; sugary rice enriched with saffron and dry fruits and the Doodhpak, a preparation of milk, rice and sugar added with dry fruits, raisins, and cardamom.

Shaak-Sabzi or Vegetables: Potato – also known as _batata' is used very commonly and finds its use in many mouthwatering dishes , like batata nu shaak. Bottle Gourd, also known as 'dudhi' is both nutritious and perennial. Mainly a summer staple, this is one vegetable that is served in a variety of ways! It can be used to make koftas, muthias (steamed dumplings) and the famous Dudhi Halwa. Shhak- an assemblage of different fried vegetable preperations include kobi batata nu shaak (caabage with green peas), tuvar ringam nu shaak (brinjal with tuvar beans), tameta batata nu shaak (tomato and potato) etc.

- Pointed Gourd: Also known as 'parwal', this gourd is cooked in variety of ways such as a curried, stir fried, sautéed with other vegetables and also stuffed!

- Karena or bitter gourd is used in the preparation of some of the tempting dishes like Karela nu saak, Bharwaan karela, Kaju karela.

- Bhinda or Okra or Lady Finger: Also known as 'bhindi', this is a seasonal summer staple in Gujarat. Unlike other regional cuisines where it is prepared as a dry, side dish, here in Gujarat, okra is served curried too.

- Gawaar or Gwaar (cluster beans) is prepared in every household in the villages, The common is Gawar nu sabzi.
- Sakariyum or Sweet Potato or Shakarkandi: This large, potato like tuberous vegetable is starchy and sweet tasting, a flavour that matures when the vegetable is cooked. It is a key ingredient of the famous dish, 'oondhiya'.
- Ringaṇa or Brinjal or Aubergines: This is yet another perennial vegetable and is available in a variety of shapes and sizes all of which have a special cooking method in Gujarati cuisine. In Gujarati food, aubergines are curried, stir fried, deep fried with batter and stuffed too.
- Pulses or Dals: Tuvar dal, Moong dal, chora or Chola (black eyed beans), Urid (Black Gram), Gwar dana, Masoor, Chana (chick peas) and mixed dal are some of the top lentils/pulses prepared in Gujarat.

Vaghar or Tempering: One word you will most likely hear in every Gujarati rasoi is Vaghar. Known as tempering in English and tadka in Hindi, using this cooking technique under-scores the flavour of the dish that is being cooked and brings out its distinct taste. Gujarati vaghar is unique and quite dissimilar to the north Indian tadka, thanks to the pronounced use of mustard seeds. To prepare vaghar, heat oil, add mustard, fenugreek and cumin seeds, and asafetida and allow it to simmer. When the seeds splutter, pour the vaghar on top of the dish you are cooking, and mix it to absorb the flavour, and instantly transform it from bland and generic to mouth-watering and quintessentially Gujarati. Vaghar is used during the preparation of staples such as dal and vegetable-based dishes, which are cooked on a day-to-day basis. It is even used as garnish for snacks such as dhokla and khandvi, amongst others.

Gujarati Thali: The classic thali of Gujarat is a wholesome platter of several authentic Gujarati delicacies served together on a large silver plate; i.e. 'thali'. The food presented on the plate depicts an enticing assortment of colors and textures and also encompasses a vast range of tastes and flavors. Variety in texture ranges from wet to dry, from granular to smooth, from coarse to grainy. Variety in colors consists in almost all the colors of a rainbow ranging from the green of veggies, yellow of the turmeric, red of the tomatoes, brown of the pulses, whiteness of the yoghurt-based dishes and the like. The vast assortment of tastes that the thali consists in includes tastes like sweet, bitter, sour and hot. Thali is actually a meal enjoyed in the company of a vast array of chutneys, pickles, and raw veggie salads.

The various items in a typical Gujarati thali may be listed as follows:

- Green vegetable
- Farsans (fried snack and steamed snack like Khakras, Dhebras)
- Gourd shaak or tuber (vegetable and spice mix in a dry or watery curry form)
- Kathol (braised pulses such as dry peas, chickpeas, beans)
- Dahi Kadhi; a yoghurt-based pulses soup
- Steamed rice/Khichdi (rice & lentil soup)
- Dal (Tuvar dal)
- Raita/Sweet Shrikhand
- Desserts (Shirkhand, halwas, basundi)

- Breads like Bajra rotla, wheat rotla, bakhris, theplas, paranthas, puris (it could be the spicy masala puri)
- Salads dressed with vinegar/curd
- Chutneys and Pickles
- Papads

CHAPTER TWENTY-ONE

Gujarati Kitchen Equipments and Utensils

Gujarati Kitchen Equipments and Utensils:

- One or two deep boiling vessels for boiling rice and other foods. Rice need only be boiled in one utensil. The taste of the rice when you boil it next will not be the same if one boils anything else in it, as oily residue from curries or other foods will be left in the rice utensil. Having to remove oily residue is not a problem, it is the taste that could change because of the residue that is off greater concern.
- Boiling vessels are necessary for lentils and pulses.
- Different pans are required for frying. This is important because of the fact that a lot of things need to be fried in Guajarati cuisine, the masalas and even some of the lentils and vegetables too.
- Strainers, drainers and stirring spoons are also required. Strainer spoons are handy, as they are porous, and help in separating solid portions of gravies.

- In addition to the above, a tawa is very important for frying chapatti and roti of different kinds.

CHAPTER TWENTY-TWO

Festive Dishes of Gujarat

FARSANS (Snack Items):

- **Dhokla:** This snack is a typical example of Gujarati food's blend of sweet, salty, spicy and sour. Made with a fermented batter of gram flour (chickpea flour), this is a steamed dish, once ready it is tempered with mustard seeds and curry leaves.

- **Patra:** Spicy gram batter stuffed calocasia leave, fried or steamed and served with chutney and pickles.

- **Khakhra:** Is a crispy flatbread that is seasoned with a variety of flavors from spices to chilies to simply salt and asafetida. The dough is made with wheat flour, much like a 'roti', except a 'khakra' is rolled out very thin and roasted on a 'tava' with very little oil, so it turns out crunchy and dry.

- **Ganthiyaa:** Cylindrical shape, fried spicy gram-flour snacks, thicker than sev.

- **Khandvi:** This is a savoury made of gram flour and curd, tempered with mustard seeds. A paste is made with the flour and then cooked slowly till it is thick. This paste is then steamed to make sheets which are lightly and delicately rolled. The rolls are then tempered; they are sometimes served stuffed too.

- **Ragdaa**: Fried spicy potato nuggets served with sev.
- **Muthiya**: Famous for both fried and steamed snacks, this is another steamed specialty from Gujarat. This recipe combines vegetables and gram flour to form dough that is formed into balls and steamed. Seasoned with cumin, aniseed, ginger and chilies, the dish is made more flavorful with a tempering of mustard seeds and asafetida.

Shaak and Daal: Vegetables and Curries:

Gujarati Kadhi: This version of 'kadhi' is made with sour curd and gram flour, thickened over a slow flame till cooked. The main difference is that it is 'sweet' yet served as a savory main course. It turns out rich and creamy with a fine sweet and sour balance.

Oondhiyu: This is a famous Gujarati main course dish made with a variety of vegetables like brinjals, potatoes, yam etc. and fenugreek dumplings which is then cooked in an aromatic blend of spices.

Batata nu shaak: Spicy potato preparation.

Trevti Daal: As the name suggests this is a lentil preparation made with three types of 'dals', moong, toor and chana. Cooked with flavours of onions, tomatoes, ginger and chillies, once ready it is tempered with red chillies and asafoetida fried in pure 'ghee'.

<u>Breads:</u>

Rotlo: Made with millet flour (bajraa) or Juwar (sorghum), these Gujarati 'roti's'are hearty and nutritious. Sometimes seasoned with spices and seasonings, these can be made stuffed too.

Bhakhri: This is a round, unleavened flatbread, much like a 'roti', except it is rolled fairly thin and turns out crisp not soft. It is served with curd, chutney, vegetables and rice. Like breads around the world, bhakri is a staple food. It is made mostly from wheat flour, jowar flour, bajra flour, nachni (finger millet) flour.

Puran poli: Sweet moong dal stuffed poories served with chutney.

Thepla: Theplas are spiced 'parantha's' made with whole wheat dough and usually eaten with curds and 'chunda', theplas can be enjoyed hot or otherwise. Sometimes whole cumin or sesame can be added to enhance the flavor of this meal staple.

<u>Rice dishes:</u>

Vagharelu bhaat: Boiled rice which is tempered with spicy mixture of chilies, mustard seeds, curry leaves and turmeric.

Khichdee: Rice and dal cooked in porridge form, served with Kadhi.

Khatta meetha bhaat: Sweet and sour rice preparation which contains potatoes and spices.

<u>Gujarati Sweets:</u>

Basundi: Much like 'rabri', this is a sweet dish cooked in milk, till the milk thickens and sweetens. Almonds and pistachios can be added to lend a crunch to this creamy dessert. In winters, the addition of saffron makes this a heartier dish.

Gud paapdee: Thin burfee like preparation made of wheat flour, jaggary, ghee and sprinkled with poppy seeds.

Mohan thal: It is a little tough burfee like preparation. In this besan ghee and sugar is cooked together in special way.

Shrikhand: This simple and cooling summer dessert is made with hung curd and is a specialty in Gujarat and Maharashtra. The strained yogurt is blended with sugar and flavored with cardamom and saffron. The flavors' depend on the recipe used. It is then left in the refrigerator for the sugar to dissolve and the dish to set, it is served chilled.

Khajoor pak: Burfees prepared with flesh of dates.

CHAPTER TWENTY-THREE

Fairs and festivals of Gujarat

Around more than 1000 festivals are celebrated in Gujarat—the state is known as the land of fairs and festivals. Some of these fairs and festivals are as follows:

Dangs Darbar: Dangs Darbar is the name of the annual fair held every year in Ahwa in Dang, which is most delightful districts of Gujarat and is located high in the Saputara hills, home of original tribes. This is one of the original home of the adivasis, the tribal population of Gujarat. Today this fair is called Jamabandi Darbar where thousands of tribal people flock to Ahwa from all over the district, dressed in bright colours, sounding the Shehnai, and beating their drums. Folk dances, dramas, and songs enliven the air during the festival. The occasion is filled with fragrance of different dishes mutton biriyanis (akhni), fried fish, patra, jalebis etc,

Chitra - Vichitra Mela (March) - This fair held after Holi, one of the largest purely Adivasi (tribal) fairs, is attended by around 60,000 to 70,000 tribal people. It takes place every year in the village of Gunbhakhari in Sabarkantha district, very near the borders of Rajasthan. The name of the fair is derived from Chitravirya and

Vichitraviraya, the sons of King Shantanu, who are believed to have lived there and been cured of diseases which afflicted them. The tribals dress in their customary colourful costumes with heavy jewellary. The women sing folk songs, and everyone dances on the beat of drums. Over a hundred stalls hold food and drink and sweets of various kinds like laddos, jalebis, daveli, etc.

Ravechi Fair - very year, during the month of September, the stark white salt desert of Kutch comes to life with the oncoming of the famous Ravechi fair. This festival draws a large number of crowds who are on a Hindu pilgrimage and gather from different parts of the world as one. This fair involves color filled cultural dances, folk songs performances and representation of traditional life in Gujarat. Dishes that enlighten in the fair are farsans of different kinds, and variety of sweets.

Navratri and Garba - The festival of navratri is celebrated with lots of enthusiasm in Gujarat. Garba is the traditional dance of Gujarat. The festival lasts for 10 days in which 9 days are of navratri and the last day is dussera. During navratri, the seventh day is celebrated as 'sharad purnima' and people have 'dudhpak' and puris with their usual meals especially in dinner. On usual days snacks counters are set near the garba grounds. 'Papdi no lot' is the most popular snacks during Navratri. On Dussera night, people eat 'fafda & jalebis'.

Makar Sankranti and Kite Flying Festival - The Kite Flying Festival takes place in mid of January and marks the time when the Sun's direct rays reach the Tropic of Capricorn after the winter solstice. It is celebrated with lots of folk music and dance as well as kite flying. People of Gujarat gather on terraces to fly kites of various colors to celebrate Makar Sankranti or Uttrayana, the welcome to the sun after the cold winter months. At night, kites with Chinese lanterns are flown and held aloft. Food such as Undhiya, sugar cane juice and local sweets is typically served to celebrate the day.

The Kutch Mahotsav - The 'Kutch Festival'or the 'Rann festival' is celebrated at the time of the Shiv Ratri in February or March. The centre of the festival is Bhuj in Kutch. It has crafts, fairs and folk dances and music and cultural shows, all organized by the Gujarat Tourism. Tours are also conducted out to the ruins of Dhola Vera, a city that was once a part of the Indus Valley civilization. Vada pav, Daveli, Bhel, Mesub (mysore pak), Gulab pak, Khari bhat (vagharelu masala bhaat), Rotlo, Besan gatta vegetable, Kersangri, buttermilk, Bhajiya, Churmu (choorma), and Magni fotravali dal (Split Mung bean dal) different types of chaats are among others enjoyed by the people.

CHAPTER TWENTY-FOUR

Some Classical Gujarati Recipes

Khandvi

Ingredients:

- 1 cup Gram flour (besan)
- 1 inch ginger
- 2 pinch salt
- ½ teaspoon powdered turmeric
- 1 pinch asafetida
- 3 cup buttermilk
- 2 green chili
- 3 tablespoon Refined oil
- 1 tablespoon lemon juice
- 1 teaspoon mustard seeds For Garnishing
- 2 teaspoon grated coconut
- ¼ bunch coriander leaves

Method:

- Take a glass bowl, sieve besan. Remove the seeds of green chilies and prepare ginger and green chili paste.
- Oil the reverse side of a stainless steel thali or marble table top with a little oil, to prevent the khandvi mixture from sticking and to ease the process of rolling the Khandvi.
- Mix the besan with ginger-green chili paste, salt, turmeric powder, lemon juice and buttermilk, taking care that no lumps are formed.
- In a thick bottomed pan, cook this mixture by stirring continuously, till it becomes a smooth thick batter. It takes a few minutes to get this ready. Quickly spread portions of the mixture over the oiled inverted thali or marble table top as thinly as possible while the batter is still very hot.
- When cool, cut into strips two inches wide and roll them tightly and taking care that you don't break them. Heat two tablespoons of oil and add a pinch of asafetida and mustard seeds. When they crackle / splutter, pour over the pieces.
- Serve immediately garnish with grated fresh coconut and finely chopped green coriander leaves. Goes best with coriander chutney, coriander mint chutney or garlic chutney.

Undhiyu

Ingredients:

- 10 tablespoon surti vaal
- 2 baby eggplant
- ¼ cup gram flour (besan)

- ½ cup small potatoes with skins
- 1 ½ cup fenugreek leaves (methi)
- ¼ teaspoon coriander seeds
- 1 teaspoon chili powder
- 1 ½ tablespoon sugar
- 2 ½ teaspoon ginger paste
- 1 green unripe bananas
- 2 ½ tablespoon virgin olive oil
- Refined oil as required
- Water as required
- 1 pinch baking soda
- 6 tablespoon yam
- ¼ tablespoon carom seeds
- ¼ cup whole wheat flour
- ¼ teaspoon cumin seeds
- ½ cup grated coconut
- 1 pinch asafetida
- ½ tablespoon lemon juice
- 2 ½ teaspoon crushed to paste green chili
- ¼ teaspoon powdered turmeric
- Salt as required
- 2 tablespoon toor daal
- ½ cup chopped coriander leaves

Method:

- **To make methi muthias** - For the same, take a deep bowl and mix together salt and fenugreek leaves in water and soak the leaves for about 7-8 minutes. When done, squeeze out all the water from the leaves and throw away the liquid.
- To the bowl full of soaked fenugreek leaves, add whole wheat flour, gram flour, chili powder, ginger, green chili

paste, turmeric powder along with sugar, a pinch of baking soda and 1 ½ tsp olive oil. Mix well all the ingredients and add a little water in the bowl and knead the mixture into smooth dough. When done, divide the dough into equal portions and roll each potion in between the palms into a round shape.

- Now, to fry the muthias, put a non-stick kadhai on medium flame and heat oil in it. When the oil is hot enough, add the muthias in the hot oil and deep fry them until golden brown in colour. When all the muthias are fried, transfer them on an absorbent paper to absorb the extra oil.

- Now, take peeled baby potatoes, sliced pieces of banana and small eggplants and make slits in the centre without splitting it completely. Next, Make a coconut- coriander masala by adding chili powder, sugar, grated coconut, chopped coriander, green garlic, cumin seed powder, coriander powder, green chili paste, ginger paste and salt as taste to the bowl. Mix well all the ingredients into a stuffing and by using spoon stuff this masala into the slits of eggplants, bananas and potatoes.

- Afterwards, take a large bowl and mix together the fresh surti vaal, yam, toor daal, and the remaining coconut-coriander masala. Keep the bowl aside to marinate for at least 10 minutes.

- Finally, put a pressure cooker on medium flame and heat oil in it. Add carom seeds in the cooker and saute on medium flame until they crackle. Then, add asafetida (hing) along with baking soda in the cooker, and fry for a few seconds. Now, add stuffed potatoes and eggplants in the cooker and increase the flame to high. Cover the cooker with a lid and cook all the vegetables for 2 whistles. After 2 whistles, switch off the burner and let the steam release on its own.

- Open the lid and toss the contents of the cooker, and then add the stuffed bananas along with fried methi muthias on top. Put the cooker once again on low flame and cook till the bananas are tender and soft while stirring occasionally. Transfer the dish to a serving platter and garnish with coriander leaves. Serve hot.

Gujarati Kadhi

Ingredients:

- 1 cup curd / yogurt
- 3 tbsp besan / gram flour
- ½ tsp ginger paste
- 1 tsp sugar
- 2 cup water
- 1 tbsp ghee / clarified butter
- ½ tsp mustard
- ½ tsp cumin / jeera
- ¼ tsp methi / fenugreek
- 3 clove / lavang
- 1 inch cinnamon
- 1 dried red chili
- Pinch hing / asafetida
- Few curry leaves
- 2 chili, slit
- ¾ tsp salt
- 2 tbsp coriander, finely chopped

Method:

- Firstly, in a large bowl take 1 cup curd, 3 tbsp besan, ½ tsp ginger paste and 1 tsp sugar.
- Add 2 cup water and whisk smooth without forming any lumps. Keep aside.
- Now in a large kadai heat 1 tbsp ghee and splutter ½ tsp mustard, ½ tsp cumin, ¼ tsp methi, 3 clove, 1 inch cinnamon, 1 dried red chilli, pinch hing, few curry leaves and 2 chili.
- Pour in prepared curd besan mixture and mix well.
- Keeping the flame on low, stir for 5 minutes or until the mixture comes to a boil. Else the curd might curdle.
- Continue to boil for 15-20 minutes on medium flame stirring occasionally.
- Further, add 1 cup water adjusting consistency as required.
- Also, add ¾ tsp salt and simmer for 2 minutes.
- Finally, add 2 tbsp coriander and serve Gujarati kadhi with hot steamed rice.

Sabudana Khichadi

Ingredients:

- 440 grams / 2 cups Sabudana before soaking
- 450 ml/ 2 cups water
- 2 tablespoon oil
- 1 teaspoon cumin seeds
- 3-4 curry leaves*
- ½ tablespoon grated ginger *
- 2 green chilies finely chopped *
- 2 medium sized potatoes peeled and cubed / 2 cups approx

- ½ cup roughly crushed roasted peanuts *

- Salt to taste sendha namak for upvaas (Hindu fasting).
- 2 teaspoon Sugar
- 1 tablespoon Lemon juice or to taste
- Fistful of Chopped green coriander
- Few roasted peanuts for garnish

Method:

- Place Sabudana in a colander .Wash Sabudana under cold tap water until clear water appears. This takes off most of the starch and prevents sticking.
- In a big wide bowl soak sabudana by adding just enough water to cover them . Just ¼ inch more than sabudana level.
- Soak covered for 5-6 hours , preferably overnight.
- Sabudana will fluff up after soaking.
- Do the smash test mentioned above in the tips.
- Drain off excess water if any before cooking.
- Add oil to a heavy bottom non stick pan.
- Once warm, add in the cumin seeds.
- Add in the cubed potatoes and cook on a low flame until tender, flipping it occasionally.
- Now add in the curry leaves, ginger , chopped chilies and cook for a minute more.
- Meantime, add in sugar, salt, crushed roasted peanuts and lemon juice to the sabudana bowl and mix well.
- Now add the coated sabudana to the pan , mix everything well and cook until the sabudana are a bit translucent and well coated.
- Keep stirring occasionally.
- Taste test and adjust the seasoning if needed.

- Add in lots of chopped green coriander and more peanuts.
- Serve warm with chilled yogurt.

Methi ka Thepla

Ingredients:

- 2 cups wheat flour / atta
- ¼ cup besan / gram flour
- ½ tsp kashmiri red chili powder / lal mirch powder
- 1 tsp sesame seeds / til
- ¼ tsp turmeric / haldi
- ½ tsp carom seeds / ajwain
- 1 green chili, chopped
- Salt to taste
- 1 inch ginger, grated
- 1 cup methi leaves / fenugreek leaves, finely chopped
- ½ cup curd / yogurt, fresh / sour
- Water as required, to knead dough
- 2 tsp oil
- tsp oil / ghee, for roasting

Method:

- Firstly, in a large mixing bowl take wheat flour and besan.
- Also add chili powder, turmeric, sesame seeds, carom seeds and salt.
- Additionally, add green chili and ginger.
- Now add finely chopped methi leaves.

- Give a rough mix making sure the spices are combined well.
- Furthermore, add half cup of curd and combine the dough well.
- Additionally, add some water and knead the dough.
- Knead the dough to smooth and soft texture like of chapathi dough.
- Add 2 tsp of oil and knead the dough for 5 more minutes.
- Now pinch medium sized ball dough, roll and flatten it.
- Also dust with some wheat flour.
- Further roll it in a thin circle like chapathi or paratha.
- Now on a hot tawa place the rolled thepla and cook for a minute.
- Furthermore, when the base is partly cooked, flip the methi thepla
- Also brush oil / ghee and press slightly.
- Finally, serve methi thepla with raita and pickle.

Shrikhand

Ingredients:

- Saffron (kesar) large pinch
- Yogurt 1 kilogram
- Sugar 1/3 cup
- Warm milk 2 tablespoons
- Nutmeg powder a pinch
- Green cardamom powder ¼ teaspoon
- Almonds blanched, peeled and sliced 5-6
- Pistachios blanched, peeled and sliced 8-10

Method:

- Tie the yogurt in a piece of muslin and hang it overnight over a bowl, in a refrigerator, to drain.
- Transfer the drained yogurt into a bowl. Add the sugar substitute and mix well.
- Soak the saffron in warm milk, cool and add to the yogurt mixture. Mix well.
- Add the nutmeg powder and cardamom powder; mix well and chill in the refrigerator.
- Serve chilled, decorated with the almonds and pistachios.

Patra

Ingredients:

- 2 cup gram flour (besan)
- ½ teaspoon pureed green chili
- Salt as required
- ½ teaspoon asafetida
- ½ teaspoon red chili powder
- 12 medium colocassia Leaves
- ½ teaspoon sesame seeds
- ½ teaspoon ginger paste
- Refined oil as required
- 1 teaspoon powdered turmeric
- ½ teaspoon mustard seeds
- ½ teaspoon tamarind paste
- ¼ cup jaggery
- Water as required

Method:

- To prepare this recipe, grate the jaggery in a small cowl and keep it aside. Now, take a separate bowl and add gram flour, ginger-chili paste, turmeric, red chili powder, ½ teaspoon asafetida, jaggery, oil and tamarind paste to it.
- Now add water along with salt and mix well until it turns into a smooth paste. On the other hand, wash the colocasia leaves and place them on a chopping board. With the help of a knife, carefully remove the veins from the center of the leaves.
- Next, apply the besan mixture on one leaf and place another leaf over it. Make sure that the mixture is evenly coated. Continue this procedure with other leaves.
- Now carefully roll the leaves and steam in a steamer for about 20 minutes. When it cools down, cut the leaves into 1 inch slices.
- Heat oil in a pan over medium flame and add mustard seeds to it. Now add the remaining asafetida along with sesame seeds and wait for them to crackle.
- Now add the Patras and gently sauté them for a minute. Serve hot with any chutney of your choice. You can even garnish it with fresh coriander leaves.

Bhendi Sambhariya

Ingredients:

- ¼ kg tender okra/bhindi/bendakayalu
- 1 tbsp oil
- ¼ tsp hing/asafetida
- few curry leaves (optional) For stuffing:
- 1 ½ tsp ginger green chili paste

- ½ tbsp roasted coriander powder
- 1 tsp roasted cumin powder
- Pinch garam masala powder
- ½ tbsp white sesame seeds
- 3-4 tbsps fresh coriander leaves, finely chopped
- 3 tbsps fresh coconut, grated
- 2 tsps brown sugar or jaggery or white sugar
- 2 tbsps coarsely powdered peanuts
- ½ tbsp oil
- Salt to taste

Method:

- Mix all the ingredients meant for stuffing in a bowl. Keep aside.
- Wash and pat dry bhindi. Make a slit length wise in each bhindi (as shown in the image above) and stuff 1 ½ tbsps of stuffing in it.
- Stuff all the bhindi and keep aside.
- Heat oil in a vessel. Once hot, add asafetida and curry leaves and sauté for few seconds.
- Add the stuffed okra and spread them around the vessel in a single layer. Add any leftover stuffing and cook on low medium flame without lid. Every few minutes turn the okra to allow even cooking on all sides. Slow roasting of the okra can take at least 30 minutes.
- Turn off heat. Serve with rice or roti.

Batata nu Saak

Ingredients:

- ½ cups peeled Potato cubes
- ¼ teaspoon Mustard Seeds (rai)
- ½ teaspoon Cumin Seeds (jeera)
- 2 teaspoons Green Chili-Ginger Paste
- 1 Tomato, chopped
- 1 pinch Asafetida
- ½ teaspoon Turmeric Powder (haldi)
- 1 teaspoon Red Chili Powder (lal mirch)
- 2 teaspoons Cumin-Coriander Powder (dhaniya-jeera powder)
- 1 teaspoon Sugar (optional)
- 2 tablespoons Cooking Oil
- 1½ tablespoons Fresh Coriander Leaves, chopped
- 1¼ cups Water
- Salt

Method:

- Heat oil in a heavy bottomed pan or kadai. Add mustard seeds; when they begin to crackle, add cumin seeds and asafetida followed by green chili-ginger paste. Stir and mix well.
- Add cubed potatoes and sauté for 3-4 minutes.
- Add chopped tomatoes, salt and sugar and sauté for 3 minutes.
- Add red chili powder and turmeric powder and sauté for 1 minute.
- Add 1¼ cups water and let mixture boil over medium flame. When boils, cook covered on medium to low flame until potatoes are cooked, stir every 4-5 minutes.
- It would take around 10-15 minutes to cook completely. If required, add more water and cook for few more minutes. (Time and water required may vary according

to type of potatoes and thickness of pan.)

- Add cumin-coriander powder, mix well. Turn off the heat. Transfer it to a serving bowl, garnish with fresh coriander leaves and serve.

Khichdi

Ingredients:

- 2/3 cup Rice (short grained)
- 1/3 cup Moong Dal (split green gram with skin) or Toor Dal (split yellow lentils)
- 3½ cups Water
- 1/8 teaspoon Turmeric Powder
- Salt to taste
- For Tadka (vaghar)
- 4-5 Garlic Cloves, chopped
- ¼ teaspoon Mustard Seeds
- ½ teaspoon Cumin Seeds
- 4-5 Curry Leaves
- ½ teaspoon Red Chili Powder
- 1 teaspoon Cumin-Coriander Powder, optional
- 1 tablespoon Oil

Method:

- Rinse rice and moong dal in water. Drain the water and transfer them to a pressure cooker (3-5 liter capacity). Add 3½ cups water, turmeric powder and salt. Mix well and taste the water for salt and add more if required.
- Close the lid and pressure cook for 4-whistles, cook on high flame until first whistle is completed and then

reduce the flame to medium. Cook over medium flame for remaining three whistles. Turn off the flame. Do not open the lid until pressure releases naturally (opening the lid immediately will result in uncooked khichdi). Open the lid after about 20 minutes and stir and mix the cooked khichdi with a spoon or spatula.

- Heat 1-tablespoon oil in a small tempering pan. When oil is medium hot, add mustard seeds. When they start to pop, add cumin seeds, chopped garlic cloves and curry leaves. When garlic starts to turn light brown, turn off the flame (It will start to turn light brown within 30-40 seconds). Add red chili powder and cumin-coriander powder and mix well.
- Pour tempering (tadka/ vaghar) over cooked khichdi and mix with a spoon. Vaghareli khichdi is now ready to serve. Serve it with plain curd and papad.

Kathiwadi Adad Dal

Ingredients:

- 1 cup White Urad Dal
- 2 Tomatoes chopped
- 1 teaspoon Ginger Garlic Paste
- Green Chilies slit
- ½ teaspoon Turmeric powder
- Lemon juice to taste
- Curry leaves a few
- Coriander Leaves, a small bunch, chopped
- Salt to taste
- To Temper
- 2 teaspoons Ghee

- 1 teaspoon Mustard seeds
- ½ teaspoon Cumin seeds
- 1 pinch Asafetida
- ½ teaspoon Red chili powder

Method:

- Wash urad dal and add in a pressure cooker, along with about 4 cups of water and turmeric. Pressure cook on medium high heat for a whistle or two, till the dal is almost mushy. Get prep with all other ingredients as well, while the dal is cooking. Once the dal is pressure cooked, allow the cooker to release pressure by itself.
- Once the pressure in the cooker is released, open the lid and mash the dal with a masher/ladle/hand blender. Keep this aside.
- In a saucepan, heat cooking oil/ghee on a medium heat. Once hot, add the mustard seeds and allow it to crackle. Once they crackle, add the cumin seeds and allow them to sizzle.
- Immediately add in the hing (asafoetida) and curry leaves and allow the curry leaves to splutter for a couple of seconds.
- To the saucepan, add ginger garlic paste, and green chillies, fry for about 1-2 minutes on medium heat or till the raw smell disappears.
- Add chopped tomatoes, red chilli powder, and salt and saute till tomatoes are mushy.
- Now add the mashed urad dal, remaining salt and turn the heat to high. Bring to a rolling boil.
- Once everything is combined well, switch off heat, add lemon juice and coriander leaves . Stir well to combine and serve.

Bhakri

Ingredients:

- 350 gm jowar flour
- Water as required
- 1 tablespoon ghee
- 2 teaspoon sesame seeds

Method:

- To prepare this Maharashtra recipe, make stiff dough of flour with water. Knead it well.
- Take small sized dough, make a ball out of it and place it on a plastic sheet.
- Wet your hands with water and pat the dough gently into a thick, flat disk. Make sure that the dough does not stick while patting.
- Heat a griddle and place the disk on it. Sprinkle some sesame seeds and roast it well.
- When the bottom of the dough turns crispy brown, turn it over and cook the other side. When it is done, serve after putting some ghee.

CHAPTER TWENTY-FIVE

Summary

Set against the backdrop of the arid and extreme climatic condition of the Thar region, Rajasthan faces the problem of scarcity of water and green vegetables. Thus, they have evolved a unique cooking style and diverse food habits that that is noticeably different from other Indian cuisines. The Rajasthanis have molded their culinary styles in such a way that many of their dishes can be shelved for several days and served without heating.

Traditionally the locals prefer to prepare such items that could be retained for a few days and consumed without heating them. Paucity of water in the region has witnessed extensive use of dairy products by the inhabitants like milk, butter and butter milk so as to compensate or reduce the water content while cooking. Ghee is liberally used in preparing different Rajasthani dishes which are rich in spice and flavor. Beans like Ker, Sangri, dried lentils and legumes like gram flour, bajra and jowar form the main ingredients are utilized quite liberally and can be seen in many Rajasthani dishes. Gram flour is one of the key ingredients that are used to cook some of the lip smacking Rajasthani food such as Pakodi, Gatte Ki Sabzi and Khata. Mangodi and Papad prepared from powdered lentils would also be a treat for your taste buds.

In many regions of the State of Rajasthan, Bajra and corn are utilized to prepare delicacies such as Khichdi, Rabdi and Rotis. Although predominantly a vegetarian region, the influence of the Rajputs who savoured non- vegetarian dishes including game meat saw the evolution of several luscious non- vegetarian dishes such as Laal maas, Jungle maas, Khad khargosh and Safed maas. Rajasthan is most famous for Dalbati - A dish comprising of dal and wheat flour kneaded with yoghurt and dressed in ghee and is generally accompanied by Churma. It is also famous for Kachori - the kachori in Rajasthan are of two types - sweet and spicy. The spicy kachori is called the pyaaz or onion kachori, and the sweet kachori called the mawa kachori. Both these kachoris are easily available in any food stalls in Rajasthan. Ghewar and Gheriya are some delectable sweet dishes originating from Mewar, available in most restaurants at Rajasthan.

Food of Gujarat is the oldest culinary treasure of India and is influenced by Vaishnavism and Jainism. The state offers a variety of vegetarian dishes including different kinds of pickles, farsans, chutneys and foods that are always high on nutrition quotient. In the cuisines of Gujarat, one can see that there is excessive of sugar, tomatoes and lemon. The reason behind this is that Gujarat is a coastal state, weather remains hot and dry throughout the year and all these ingredients keep the body hydrated. Cuisines of Gujarat have emerged from the different communities who have settled in the state. Gujarat is divided into four regions- North Gujarat, Kathiawad, Kutch, and South Gujarat. In all these regions, different types of cuisines are cooked because of their climatic conditions.

North Gujarat is prominent for its thalis. Farsans (snacks) including items like khaman, khandvi, kachori, mini-samosa, dhokla, and dahi vada are the specialty of North Gujarat thali. South Gujarat cuisine is known for its use of chilies in almost every dish. Undhiyu and Paunkh are few popular dishes that are served in South Gujarat.

Even the cuisine of Khathiawad is known for its spicy quotient as there is excessive use of chilies here as well. Dhebras (prepared with wheat flour, yoghurt, spinach, green chilies, sugar and salt) served with Chhunda (sweet and sour mango pickle) is loved by the people of Khathiawad region. In North Gujarat and south Gujarat, one can find flavorful delicacies but in Kutch the scenario is a little bit different as a simple meal is served. The main dish of Kutch region is the Khichdi and kadhi or Bajra no rotlo, guvarnu shaak.

A typical thali that contains many small bowls filled with curries, snacks, sides, sweets, bread, chutney (spicy condiment) and pickles. Distinctive things about Thali is that it allows you the savory the delicate balances of flavor-sweet, salty, spicy, crisp, soft, fried and deep fried. Bread include the Rotlis (baked bread) made from Bajra (millets) and the Thepla (griddled bread made of chickpea). Khichdi (a mixture of rice and five kinds of lentils), Kadhi (preparation of sweet and spicy curd mixture thickened with gram flour), Masala Bhat (spiced rice) and Vangi Bhat (rice with aubergines and coriander). Jaggery often paired with rice is served as a sweet. Sweet delicacies include seasonal Aamras (mango fool) and Dhoodh Pake, made with thick sweetened milk, dried gruits and nuts. For the snacks, there are crisp Farsans, particularly Dhokla(spongy cake made of chickpea flour and yoghurt), Khandvi (chickpie rolls filled with cocnut slices), Mirchi Pakoda (fried snacks made of chili pepper) and Khakra (wafers). Also not to forget are the Nankhatais (local biscuits of

Gujarat). With all the species, herbs and the flavors, cuisines of Gujarat are worth relishing.

CHAPTER TWENTY-SIX

Glossary

- Aanch: This is a cooling Indian summer drink made with unripe green mango pulp. It is also called aam panna It is slightly sour and sweet to taste and is flavored with cumin jeera, mint leaves and black salt. All ingredients are blended together to make the refreshing drink.

- Basundi: This is a rich, delicious and flavorful Indian sweet made by thickening full fat milk and sugar. It is then garnished with nuts. Basundi is mostly popular in the Western Indian states of Maharashtra, Gujarat and some parts of Karnataka. It can be served on its own chilled and garnished with nuts or with Poori. A close variation to this is Rabri or rabdi made in North India. However they both differ in the texture and consistency. Traditionally basundi is made by simmering full fat milk for a long time until the milk reduces to almost half the original quantity.

- Bhakhri: This is typically round flat unleavened Gujarati biscuit-like bread flavored with ghee and cumin seeds. Generally, there are two types of bhakhris—one is cooked like a biscuit while the other is puffed up and served with ghee. A simple Roti also said to be Bhakari, in various places of Maharashtra.

- Chilla: These are simple spiced gram flour pancakes from Guajarati and North Indian cuisine. These can be eaten with a chutney or enjoyed just with a cup of tea or coffee either for breakfast or evening snack. Common example is Besan ka cheela.
- Chullah: It is a kind of clay stove used for cooking the food using wood or cowdung cake or charcoal fuel.
- Dabeli: Dabeli is a renowned street food available mainly on the streets of Gujarat. Dabeli is also called as Kutchi Dabeli or Kachchhi Dabeli. basically Dabeli is a spicy, tangy and sweet potato filling inside a bun more specifically the Indian bun; called as pav, drizzled with a spicy and sweet chutney and some pomegranate, grapes, onions and sev (fried gram flour vermicelli).
- Diljani: Diljani is a dessert made from gram flour, sugar syrup, clarified butter, saffron and dried fruits. The process of making this delicious dessert is similar to the way boondi is prepared. Once the gram flour balls are fried, they are soaked into sugar and saffron syrup and later on orange syrup (optional).
- Dudhpak: Doodhpak is a Guajarati rice pudding made from milk, rice, sugar, saffron and nuts. Dudhpak is commonly accompanied by poori. The milk is slow-boiled to thickened and sweetened and the dish is garnished with chopped almonds and pistachios.
- Gharis: It is a sweet Gujarati dish from Surat. Ghari is made of puri batter, milk 'mawa', ghee and sugar - made into round shapes with sweet filling, to be consumed on Chandani Padva festival. It is also available in many varieties and flavors such as pistachio, almond-elachi and mawa.

- Ghevar: It is a crispy deep fried disc-shaped sweet cake with porous texture and is mainly served by dipping it in sugar syrup or topped with milk rabdi. It's a special sweet for the festival of Teej and Rakhsha Bandhan.
- Gotma: This is mashed small sweet boondis.
- Jhanajariya: It is a delicacy made of maize or corn, milk, ghee and sugar garnished with raisins and nuts. Grated or coarsely ground fresh sweet corn is slowly roasted in ghee for few hours until it loses most of its moisture and assumes a dry granular form.
- Khad: It is a baked meat recipe from Rajasthan's royalty. A spiced mix of minced lamb and potato is layered with phulkas and baked golden in oven or covered Bhatti.
- Laapsi: This is a traditional dish of Rajasthan and Gujarat prepared with porridge (broken wheat). Lapsi is often prepared for some special occasions or for rituals (puja). This dish is really delectable to eat.
- Mesub: It is a popular Gujarati sweet made especially during festivals such as Diwali. Also known as Mysore pak in Karnataka.
- Muthiya: It resembles sausage, or any disc shape and is made up of besan, methi (fenugreek), salt, turmeric, chili powder, and an optional bonding agent/sweetener such as sugar and oil. It is a staple of Guajarati.
- Oondhiyu: This is a traditional Gujarati style of making mixed vegetable curry that is a regional specialty of Surat city.
- Panchkuta: This curry dish is essentially made up of 5 ingredients found widely across the Great Thar Desert which are Ker, Sangri, Amchur, Gunda and Kumati . It has a long shelf life after being cooked and does not require refrigeration, unlike other foods.

- Phafda: This is a fried crispy crunchy tasty snack made with besan (gram flour), laced with carom (ajwain) seeds and black pepper. A popular Gujarati snack.
- Raabori: An asafoetida-infused sundried millet flour/ buttermilk/ poppadum and leeks concoction that simply melts in the mouth.
- Rasowara: Rajasthani royal kitchen.
- Ringna no oroh: Ringna No Oroh is char roasted brinjal delicately flavored with ginger and spices. Ringna No Oroh is a classic dish made from roasted brinjals and when combined with green chillies, ginger and spices they release flavors that are absolutely delectable. This dish known as Baingan Bharta in some regions of India.
- Rotlo: A traditional Gujarati flat-bread recipe of black millet or bajra served best with baingan bharta.
- Shrikhand: This is the traditional sweet from Gujarat and Maharashtra. It is also known as 'Matho'. It is made from hung or strained curd/yogurt and sugar. Cardamom and chopped nuts are also added.
- Sohan halwa: It is a traditional dessert of Rajasthan and Gujrat. It is made by cooking cornflour, ghee, sugar and nuts together till thick. Then it is cut into burfee shape.
- Surti locho: It is steamed Gujarati Farsan (snack /side dish) originated in Surat and is a traditional street food . It is made from gram flour. The dish derives its name from its loose consistency and irregular shape like dumplings. It is served with spicy desi chutney, chilies and sev.
- Tikkad: Tikkad is a typical Rajasthani spicy corn bread eaten especially in the Thar region. It is thick, spicy, and very very rustic. Very similar to missi roti.
- Tikra: Rotis stuffed with spiced papad mixture.

- Trevti daal: Trevti Dal is a classic Gujarati recipe which is cooked using three different lentils. The lentils are tempered with mild spices making Gujarati style creamy lentils simple yet delectable. Generally Chana dal, moong dal and Arhar dal is preferred.
- Vaghar: It is the term used for tempering.

CHAPTER TWENTY-SEVEN

Reference and Acknowledgements

<u>Reference and Acknowledgements:</u>

- Gujarat Tourism (Official website)
- Rajasthan Tourism (Official website)
- India Tourism (Official website)
- Lonely Planet, India – Travel Guide (Book)
- Be your Own Guide to Indian Cookery – Dr Anshumali Pandey (Book)
- History of Indian Cookery – Dr Anshumali Pandey (Book)

The Author

Dr. Anshumali Pandey is a renowned & reliable name in the field of Education, Hospitality, Tourism and Tribal Food. He is a Teacher and Chef by profession, and also an Author, a Business Auditor, and an avid culinary traveller to the Indian Sub continental hinterlands. Dr. Anshumali Pandey is a Hospitality Educator (PhD) who specialises in Higher Education, Office Administration, Pay roll, HR, Labour Laws, Audit, and Procurement & Tender Process. He is an Author with 65 Publications consisting of 47 Books.

His contribution and research in the field of Tribal Food, Tribal Tourism, Forest Tourism and Village Tourism in the form of research papers have brought several laurels to him. In 2018 the Ministry of Tourism, Govt of Indian duly recognised all this and awarded him with a National

Appreciation certificate and memento.

The books written by **Dr Anshumali Pandey** are essentially a banquet arising from an experience of over 25 years of Professional life and have boiled down to crisp and accurate writing on his favourite subjects. Hospitality Sector champion requires to be a specialist in many fields and Dr Pandey is one of them. His knowledge is evident from the spectrum of subjects which he has chosen for his books so far, which ranges from being a specialist chef, to Master of Human resources, to Education and to love for children, and topped with Spirituality. For more than two decades Dr Pandey has lived with his family in Western India in general and the Tribal belt of the union territory of Dadra & Nagar Haveli in particular. Most of his time is consumed in helping and understanding the Tribal and rural population of the region and writing scholarly articles and books on his vast area of interest.

Books written by the Author are –

1. Theory of Indian Cookery
2. Beauty and Irony of Silvassa Tourism
3. A Short Indian Food Story
4. Be Your Own Guide to Indian Cuisine
5. Cookery Fundamentals
6. History of Indian Food (2 Editions Printed)
7. The Great Indian Story Book for Children
8. Personal Budget: Easy Work Book
9. Online Classes Log Book
10. Dictionary Making Work Book for School Children
11. The Lazy Bed
12. Hindu Dharm (हिन्दू धर्म) (In Hindi Language)
13. Where is my coffee?

14. Your First Job is Never your Last (Volume 1)
15. You are Almost There (Quick Fix Resume and Interview Hacks)
16. Working for the Enemy? - A lesson in Career Management
17. Public Speaking for the Young
18. A Date With Coffee
19. How to be The Best Hotel Front Office Employee
20. Diploma in Food Production, The complete Syllabus
21. Diploma in F&B Service, The Complete Syllabus
22. Diploma in Front Office, The Complete Syllabus
23. The Time to Speak is Now
24. Munshi Premchand (Short Stories in English)
25. The Housekeeping Department, Text Book
26. Hitchhiker's Guide to Trekking in Uttarakhand
27. Uttarakhand, A divine Land for a Reason
28. Bachhon ke liye rochak kahaniyan (बच्चों के लिए रोचक कहानियाँ) (In Hindi Language)
29. Basic Communication Skills of English
30. The Basic Office Organisation Book for Start-ups
31. Hospitality HRM
32. Hospitality Marketing
33. Bakery Ingredients and Tools
34. Human Resource Management for Indian Professionals
35. The process of LAWFULLY operating a Hospitality business in India
36. Indian Classical Sweets: History, Tradition and Recipes
37. History of India's Himalayan Cuisine: Classical Cookery of Kashmir, Laddakh, Jammu, Himachal, Lahaul, Spiti, Garhwal, Kumaon.
38. Vindu: Andhra Cuisine (Part 1 of South Indian Trilogy)
39. Saappadu: Tamil Cuisine (Part 2 of South Indian

Trilogy)

40. Sadya: Malayali Cuisine (Part 3 of South Indian Trilogy)
41. South Indian Cuisine - The Researcher's Guide Book
42. The Ramayana for Children and other short stories from Indian Mythology
43. Legends of the Tribal Shiva
44. Third Generation Children's Story Book
45. It's Elementary: The Top Nine Adventures from the memoirs of Dr John H Watson
46. UNITY IN DIVERSITY, The foundation of Indian Tourism
47. The Thar Express: Culinary History of Rajasthan and Gujarat

Connect with me: anshumali.pandey@gmail.com
https://notionpress.com/author/337004

Please scan this QR code on you phone to know more about the latest and complete works of Dr Anshumali Pandey